TAKES HOOD OFF.

GREEN HOUSE SHIP

MORE MODEST

18

CLAY.

FRANK

cubicle too small

NAICS

YELLOW LINE

THE ART OF
Disney · PIXAR
ELEMENTAL

Foreword by **Pete Docter**   Introduction by **Peter Sohn**

CHRONICLE BOOKS
SAN FRANCISCO

FRONT COVER Lauren Kawahara and Don Shank
(layout), *digital*

BACK COVER Lauren Kawahara and Don Shank
(layout), *digital*

FRONT FLAP Yon Hui Lee, *pen and ink on paper*

BACK FLAP Yon Hui Lee, *pen and ink on paper*

ENDSHEETS Peter Sohn, *pen and ink on paper*

PAGE 1 Ralph Eggleston, *digital*

PAGES 2-3 Maria Yi, *digital*

THIS PAGE Carlos Felipe León, *digital*

Library of Congress Cataloging-
in-Publication Data is available.

ISBN 978-1-7972-1851-9

Manufactured in China.

FSC
www.fsc.org

MIX
Paper | Supporting
responsible forestry
FSC™ C008047

Design by Liam Flanagan.

10 9 8 7 6 5 4 3 2 1

Chronicle Books LLC
680 Second Street
San Francisco, California 94107
www.chroniclebooks.com

Foreword

Elemental is a story of a Fire woman who falls in love with a Water guy, and it grew directly out of Director Pete Sohn's personal experience. While it is true that Pete is 60 percent water, that's not what I'm talking about. Feeling stuck between love for family and love for a romantic partner was a pivotal experience for Pete, and telling this relatable idea with characters made out of fire, water, earth, and air made for an amazingly unique and compelling concept.

But just because you have a great idea for a film doesn't mean you can sit back and watch the awards and cash roll in. (That's a common misconception.) A wonderful concept can be carried out poorly and make everyone say, "Remind me why we thought this would be good?" That's not something you want to say after five years of work, and it's why we work so long and hard to refine our stories and characters.

This refinement process is grueling because there is no road map for what belongs in the film. Many great ideas are created, refined, and polished . . . only to be thrown out when we realize they don't really belong. Luckily, we have this book, where we can capture and show off some of our favorite explorations.

Besides the normal pathfinding, the *Elemental* team also needed to design what may be *the* most difficult characters we've ever created at Pixar Animation Studios. And that's saying something, considering we've tackled emotions, souls, and octopuses. What made it so tough? If you've ever studied fire burning, smoke drifting, or water pouring, you've noticed how different these elements look from moment to moment. Would we even be able to make characters out of something as ephemeral as fire or water? Would they be recognizable from one scene to another? And then there's the technical challenge: Organic elements are some of the most complex things you can create in computer graphics—especially if you need to control these elements, as we did, so they could act.

Fortunately for all of us, the amazing artists and technicians at Pixar like a challenge. They not only pulled it off but made it absolutely amazing, and unlike anything you've ever seen before.

And it all started with the images you'll see in this book.

Pete Docter, Chief Creative Officer

FLAME BOAT PEOPLE

Introduction

My parents have told me the story of how they immigrated to New York from South Korea at least a bazillion times. If my brother and I ever complained about something, we would hear about how they survived a war, or how they were so poor they ate grasshoppers, or how they had it so much harder in Korea than we had it here in the United States.

And as a kid, every time I heard these stories of their home, I would roll my eyeballs so hard I could've used them for bowling.

But as I grew up, I began to see all these other families that immigrated to this country going through the same things my parents went through: different cultures mixing, and sometimes not mixing, with each other to make it work. I started to actually hear what was in my parents' stories and to appreciate all the hard work it took for them to create a life here for my brother and me. That appreciation turned into a gratefulness that then turned into a deeper love, which then turned into a *cry-when-I-think-about-it, soul-crushing weight of debt that can never be repaid.*

Yup, here come the tears.

All of these feelings were the start of *Elemental*, connecting my experience to a world similar to New York—a world where Fire, Earth, Air, and Water all live on top of each other, mixing, and not mixing, and trying to create a life for themselves. One of the first drawings I did, which triggered the idea for the film, was a boat full of Fire people making a treacherous journey over water to get to that new life. How do you make all of this, you ask? Like any fire, it all started with an Ember.

The team knew our first challenge would be creating our main Fire character, and that the other Elements and environments would grow from there. But we weren't even sure we could make a character out of fire. Could we make it believable that a gaseous being of light could walk, talk, and make decisions in an appealing way? There have been many films with a realistic blaze, dragons blowing tornadoes of fire, and monsters going up in hellish flames; but real, photographed fire would look terrifying or too visually noisy for our main character. The other end of the spectrum was to try a more illustrated approach. There is a long history of beautiful hand-drawn 2D fire in animation, but for our purposes an illustrated fire could be too graphic and not feel like it was giving off heat or could burn something.

Finding a balance between these two seemingly polar-opposite styles became our solution, a yin and yang of opposite ideas that are actually interconnected—two characters from different worlds that come together and find connection. When I first pitched the idea for *Elemental*, I based some of the relationships in the story on my family, but I also based some of them on the person I fell in love with. My grandmother and my mother told me many times throughout my teenage years, "Hanguk yujah hagoo gyuranheh!" *Marry a Korean woman!* But I fell in love with someone who wasn't Korean, and that was the inspiration for the main question that started this film:

What if Fire fell in love with Water?

One of our challenges with these extremes is that the audience knows what fire and water look like. They know

how fire blooms and burns. They know how water drips and glistens. So there wasn't a lot of room for interpretation in finding a connection between the two—and on top of that, both elements are constantly moving! The characters are essentially special effects, and having every shot in a film be a special effect is very difficult. These challenges would take our team of artists and technicians over two years to uncover and ultimately solve.

Can these opposites even have a connection? One of the first experiments for this film was a small bit of animation that the talented artist Daniel López Muñoz did of Ember just blinking. It was a combination of cell phone footage he shot of real fire in his backyard mixed with an illustrated set of eyes, a mouth, and a kind of outline around Ember created from a color gradient of red to yellow. At the same time, we had a design of Wade where he had this balance of photorealist bubbles layered on top of a water-colored interior and a meniscus around his head. Wade's meniscus looked like the outline around Ember. This was the first example of a unifying connection between the two extremes, an

aesthetic balance that allowed these two to feel like they came from a similar world.

As a character, Ember becomes caught between two extremes in her life: growing up proud of her home in Firetown but also falling in love with the more diverse world of Element City. These two different parts of her identity that she struggles with are very much inspired by my own struggle with identity—growing up in New York and wanting to assimilate but not fitting in because I'm Korean, and trying to understand how these two disparate upbringings can come together. It doesn't matter where you are or how old you are when going through this process of understanding your identity; the developmental milestones are the same for many: There's wanting to assimilate into the majority culture, which then triggers a rejection of your "minority" culture. Only by growing and learning to appreciate that rejected culture will you get to a point where you begin to accept both pieces of yourself. But for Ember, it has never been one or the other. It isn't red or blue; it is purple. It is mixing those two identities and figuring out how she can be both.

ABOVE, LEFT
Don Shank, *ink and watercolor on paper*

ABOVE, RIGHT
Peter Sohn, *digital*

In this book, I hope you'll see how the artists took these challenges and created solutions for Ember and her journey through this wondrous city—finding balance throughout it all. It is a love story, after all, and I fell in love with watching all these amazing artists mix together and, through their passion and brilliance, create an immaculate world filled with diverse characters. I'll be forever grateful for the small and large sacrifices our artists made to make these miracles happen. Ember and Wade and the world of *Elemental* could never have been made with just one department or one person; the only way they came to life was through the tight collaboration of art, modeling, simulation, production, editing, effects, shading, animation, lighting, story, writing, acting, and countless more. Just more proof that diversity makes everything better.

Looking back at all the artwork in this book triggers an appreciation for these contributors. That appreciation turns into a gratefulness, which then turns into a deeper love, which then turns into a *cry-when-I-think-about-it, soul-crushing weight of debt that can never be repaid.*

Yup, tears again.

Peter Sohn, Director

Alice Lemma, Anna Scott, and Maria Yi, *digital*

Maria Yi, *digital*

Elemental-izing

Don Shank, *digital*

Don Shank, *ink on paper*

One of the major keystones to the design of the movie was this wonderful chair that our production designer Don Shank drew. It was taking the idea of something that we use with fire—a fire grate that you would put in a fireplace to hold logs— but he tilted one side of it to be the back of a chair and then distilled the bars from ten down to three. Terrible and uncomfortable for a human, but a perfect chair for a Fire character. From this, several design philosophies emerged. When trying to design something for a specific Element, we found an object from our world that we all knew and then twisted it into something new—bonus points if it was a funny twist. In addition to distilling objects down, we caricatured the shapes to be clearer. The subtle torquing Don did to the bars added a signature, and the twisting of the bars evoked an organic quality that started to unify the world.

Peter Sohn, Director

Don Shank, *color pencil and ink on paper*

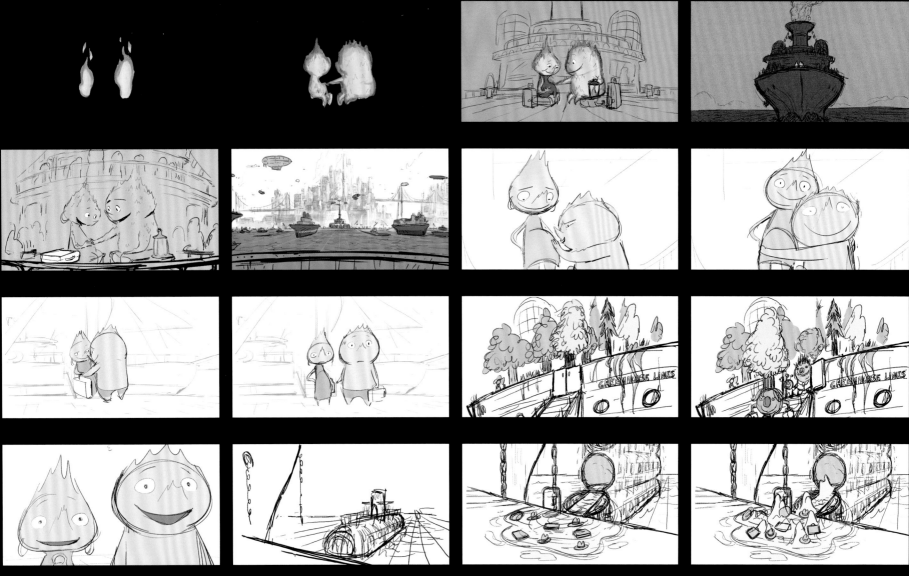

NEW ARRIVALS

Yung-Han Chang, Dan Park,
Peter Sohn, and Le Tang,
digital

Baked into the DNA of our film is an immigration story. Tales of people bravely leaving their homeland to arrive somewhere new, quite often with nothing, and building a better life for themselves and their family. Peter's own story of growing up in a first-generation household and the sacrifices his mother and father made in their journey to America were a huge inspiration way to introduce our audience to the world of Element City would be through the eyes of a pair of new arrivals. Our story attempted to encompass the hope and the challenges Bernie and Cinder share on their journey to build a new life in this unfamiliar land.

Jason Katz, Head of Story

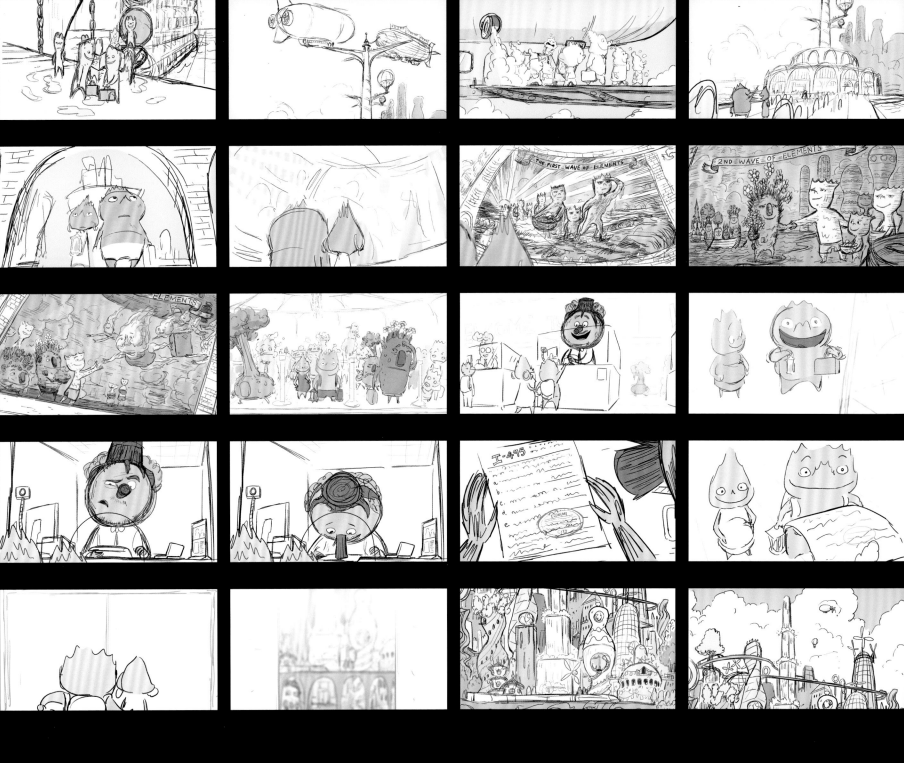

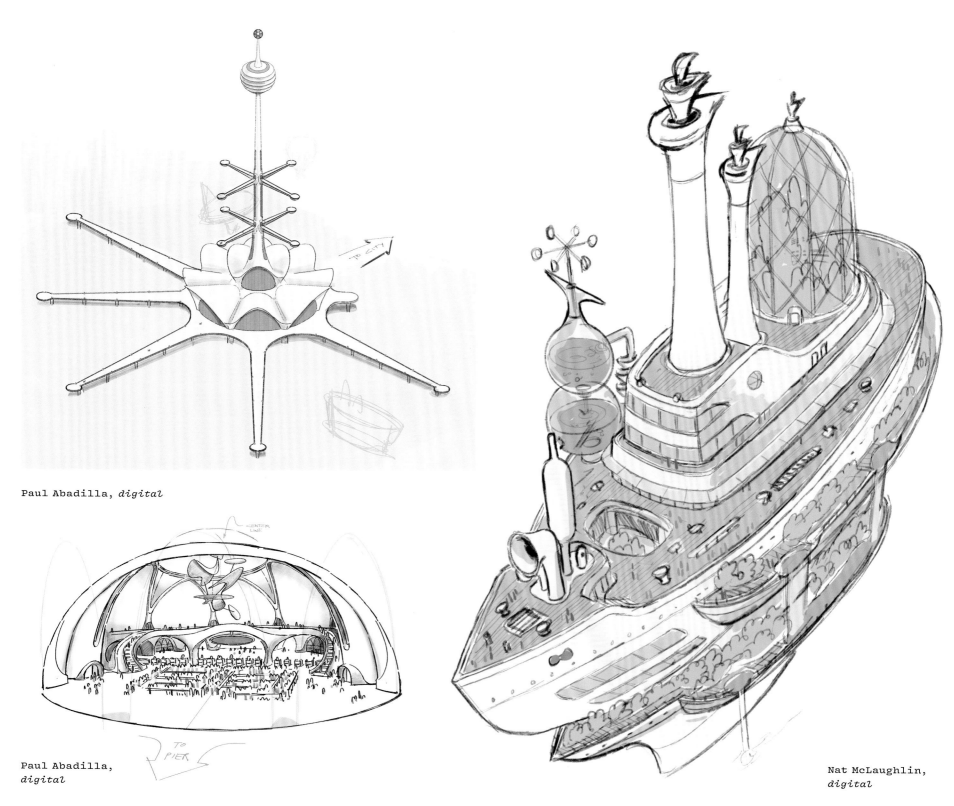

Paul Abadilla, *digital*

Paul Abadilla,
digital

Nat McLaughlin,
digital

20

Shank 4-4-2017

Element City was imagined to be founded by Water. However, we wanted it to feel like all Elements could live here, so we looked for ways of living that would suit everyone, not just one Element or the other. This way they could live mixed together. We found inspiration in chemistry sets and related instruments, then laid specific architectural structures onto that, like windmills and farm terraces. Ultimately, we dialed down the chemistry set influence, but you will still see it throughout Element City.

Don Shank, Production Designer

Don Shank, *ink and watercolor on paper*

Don Shank, *ink and watercolor on paper*

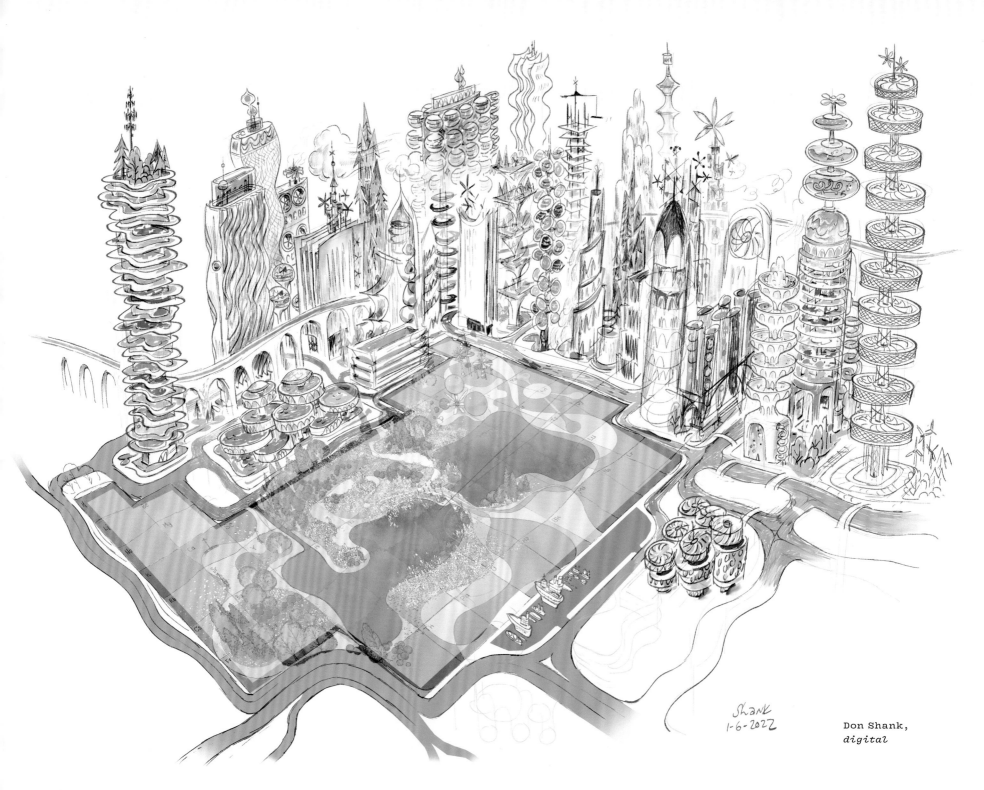

Don Shank,
digital

Lauren Kawahara and Don Shank
(layout), *digital*

24

ABOVE
Lauren Kawahara,
digital

RIGHT
Daniel Holland,
*ink and watercolor
on paper*

FAR RIGHT
Ana Ramírez Gonzáles,
*ink and watercolor
on paper*

When we started to develop the color design for Element City, our goal was to create an environment that felt hopeful and inviting, while also having a touch of whimsy and magic. At the same time, we wanted to explore how graphic light and shadow shapes could act as framing devices and how a character's light might affect a scene. Ultimately, we felt that a colorful and vibrant palette could best support and explore these ideas.

**Lauren Kawahara,
Shader Packet Designer**

Lauren Kawahara
and Don Shank (layout),
digital

Daniel Holland, *paper and wood*

Don Shank, *digital*

LEFT Jasmin Lai, *digital*

29

Hye Sung Park, *digital*

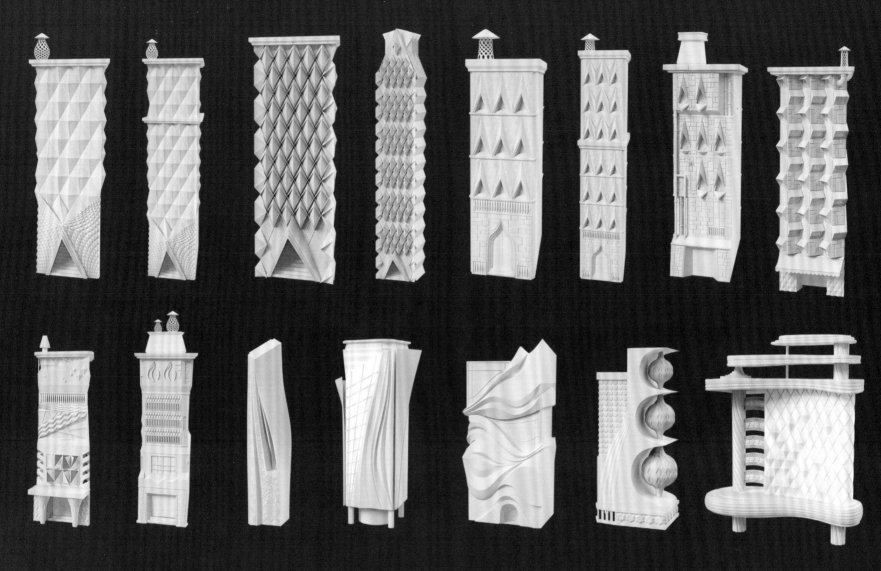

These development models by Krista Goll were instrumental in exploring our inspiration of paper sculpture and ways these ideas could manifest in our set models. We learned quite a bit from her design work here that informed our overall modeling philosophies and style guide.

Don Shank, Production Designer

Krista Goll (design model), *digital*

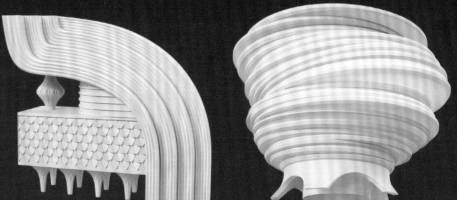

Lauren Kawahara and Don Shank (layout), *digital*

Don Shank, *digital*

Elle Michalka, *digital*

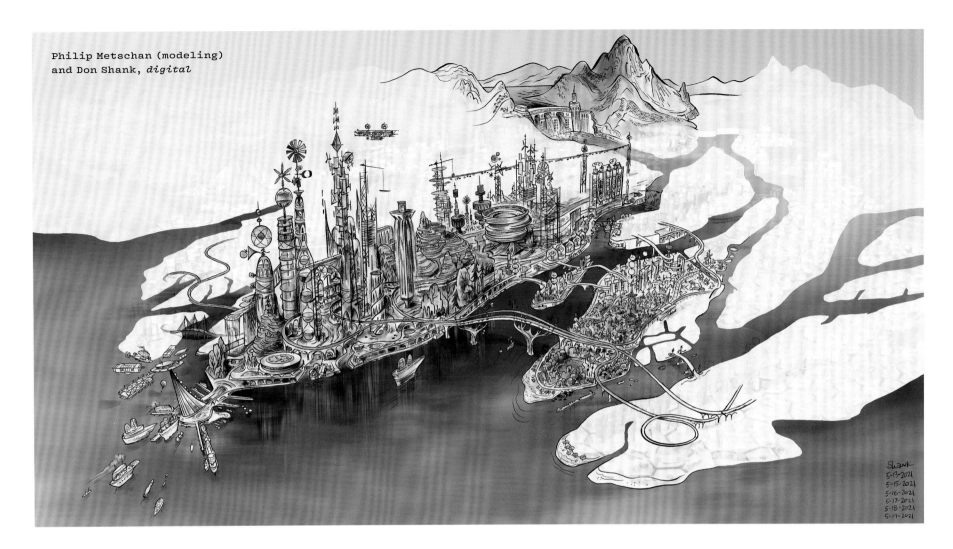

Philip Metschan (modeling)
and Don Shank, *digital*

Don Shank,
digital

When we were trying to understand the hierarchy of which Element came to the area first, we started breaking down the relationships of these communities and worked from there. For story reasons, we needed to make the world a little harder for Fire, and so a community built by Water felt like a good start. From there we thought Earth would be a logical second group to come to this area because of the symbiotic relationship of needing water to grow plants. So that's where the concept of a delta made sense: a place where there are lots of streams and tributaries cutting through the land—where water and earth meet.

Peter Sohn, Director

33

Daniel López Muñoz, *digital*

ABOVE Joshua Mills
(design model), *digital*

OPPOSITE Jasmin Lai,
digital

34

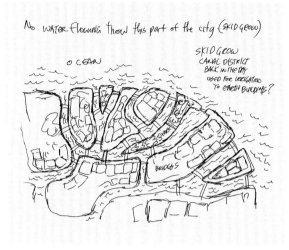

In some of my favorite romance movies, the setting where the story takes place is always heightened to be memorable and beautiful in support of the growing love between the characters. Whether it's the Golden Gate Bridge in San Francisco or the Brooklyn Bridge in New York, trying to design iconic places to reinforce what the characters were going through became a goal for us. The Element City Bridge was important to Ember because it represented a threshold between her two identities—Firetown, her home, and Element City, her possible future. Ultimately, the bridge would become who she is—that she is both from Firetown and from the city. It was designed beautifully to represent that identity.

Peter Sohn, Director

ABOVE Peter Sohn, *ink on paper*

RIGHT AND OPPOSITE Philip Metschan (design model), *digital*

Daniel López Muñoz, *digital*

36

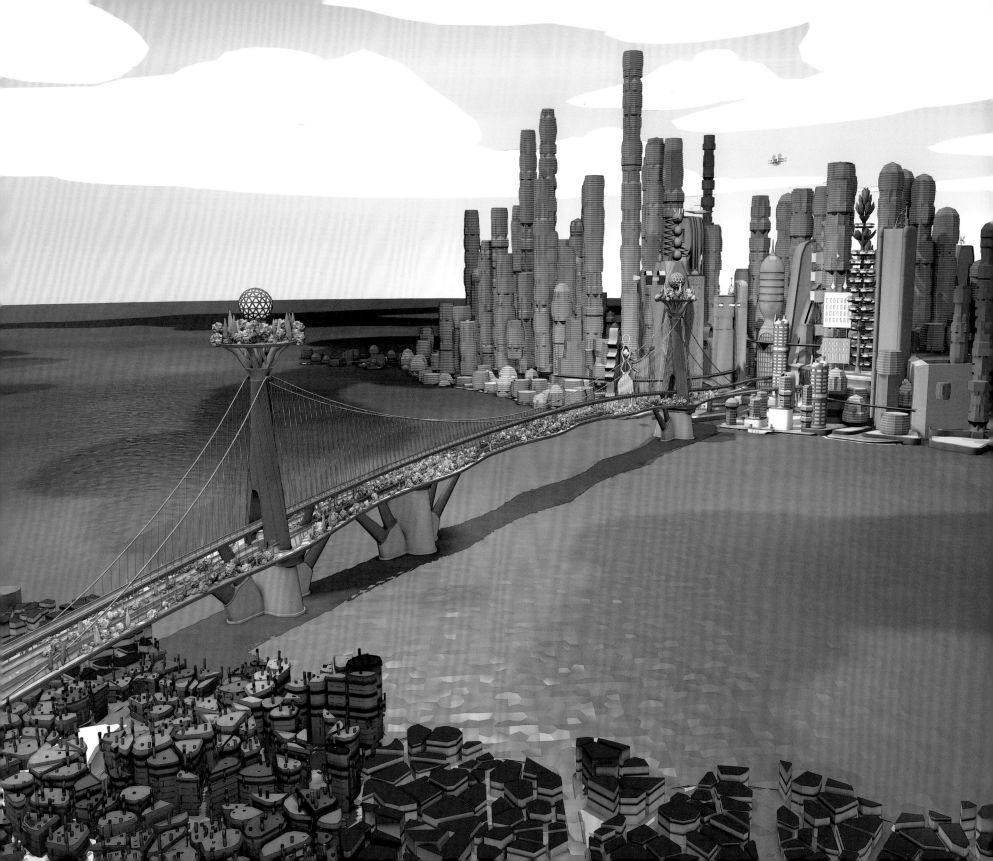

FLIPBOOK (PAGES 39–83)
Daniel López Muñoz,
digital composition

We decided early on that Ember's flame was fueled by emotions rather than true physics. However, a flame character of this complexity had not yet been made in Pixar history. And so, the paper plane animation test was born. Shown as a flipbook in the right corner of the next few pages, this hand-painted test shows that a very flammable object could penetrate Ember's head and come out believably unscathed on the other side. Pete liked this particular test because it showed the ethereal quality of her flame and that her core was all flame rather than an object caught on fire. Quickly flip through these pages to see how this test became an important milestone for creating our Fire Elements.

Daniel López Muñoz, Concept Designer

LEFT
Jason Deamer, *digital*

THIS PAGE
Maria Yi, *digital*

Daniel López Muñoz, *pencil and digital*

Designing Fire characters was definitely a learning experience for us—we wanted to create a new look of fire that feels familiar yet innovative. Initially, we approached with an extremely stylized fire design to understand the limits, then gradually found a great balance by incorporating the real qualities of fire that we were all excited about.

Maria Yi, Characters Art Director

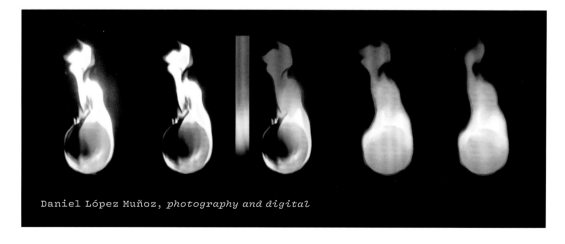

Daniel López Muñoz, *photography and digital*

THIS SPREAD
Daniel López Muñoz,
pen and digital

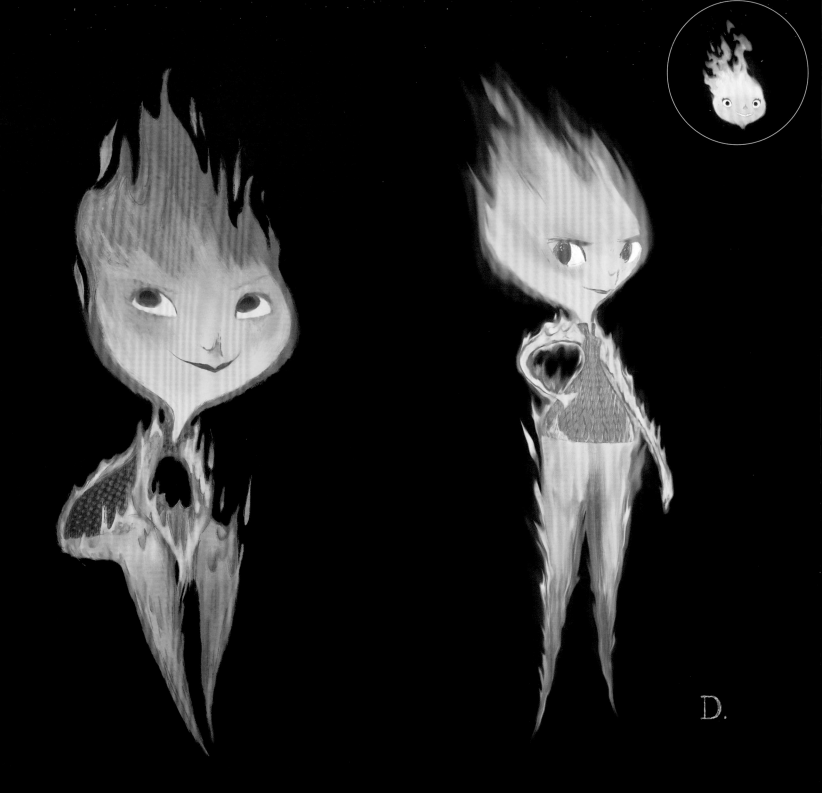

CRYING
SPARKS

Peter Sohn,
ink on paper

Maria Yi, *digital*

Maria Yi, *digital*

Finding the look of Ember was an exciting challenge; we were looking for something familiar and new at the same time. Initially, we started with something very stylized and gradually found our way to get to this painting. Pete called it "Champagne Ember" because this version captured the beautiful characteristic of fire but was playfully stylized.

Maria Yi, Characters Art Director

FAR LEFT Jonathan Hoffman, *digital*

LEFT Maria Yi, *digital*

Carlos Felipe León, *digital*

Maria Yi, *digital*

FIRE

Jeeyoon Park,
digital

Don Shank, *color pencil and ink on paper*

In translating our settings into elementalized versions, we wanted to have the architecture feel born out of the Element's culture but not just be a simple one-to-one replacement. We started by having Fire characters live in giant cooking pots but quickly moved to building architecture that was assembled with parts and pieces of recognizable, real-world items that relate to fire, water, air, or earth. Certain large silhouette ideas like the cooking pots still felt unique as a base to work from, and so we started stacking them to get taller buildings and to add an interest and complexity to the design.

Don Shank, Production Designer

Peter Sohn, *ink on paper*

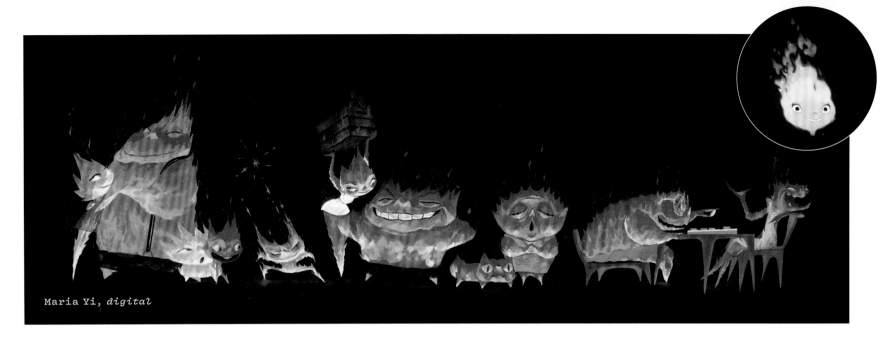

Maria Yi, *digital*

Jennifer Chia-Han
Chang, *digital*

Laura Meyer, *digital*

Daniel López Muñoz, *digital*

Daniel López Muñoz, *digital*

TENEMENT "TYPE" BUILDINGS

SPA & SAUNA

HAMMERED COPPER

"CLOCK" TOWER

KEROSENE NOZZLE "FIRE-TOWER"

BETTER "HEAT CONDITIONING" ON THE TOP FLOORS

FIRE CONDITIONING

STOVETOP B&BQ

MRS POTTERS

PETERS FIREWORKS & CO.

HARDENED MUD WITH BRICK INCLUSIONS

DOUBLE BURNER STOVE TOP "WINDOW A/C"

BRASS

CERAMIC TILE

PERHAPS SMALLER BUILDINGS ARE MORE UNIQUE

FIRE v BUILDING STRUCTURE

MORE FIRE PRESENCE · 80%

MORE SINGULAR FIRE PRESENCE · 20%

Elle Michalka, *digital*

Jennifer Chia-Han Chang, *digital*

Nat McLaughlin, *digital*

OPEN LATE **FIREWORKS** KA**BOOM** HEADQUARTERS

Laura Meyer, *digital*

Valerie Kao, *digital*

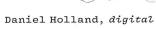

Daniel Holland, *digital*

The original concept of Firetown was it used to be an Earth neighborhood that is run down and no longer inhabited. We tried to find Fire culture architecture that was inspired by Fireland but also had new Fire-related elements that evoke bigger city buildings. We wanted The Fireplace, a leftover Earth building, to look like a triangular Flatiron-type structure, but we were also looking for something to make it iconic. Eventually Pete pointed back to an earlier elementalized concept piece where outdoor wood oven shapes were stacked on top of each other. To make them resemble apartments, we fit them together upside down to create a pattern. This was the keystone idea that gave us the feel we were after.

**Don Shank,
Production Designer**

ABOVE
Jeeyoon Park, *digital*

RIGHT
Daniel López Muñoz, *digital*

FAR RIGHT
Jennifer Chia-Han Chang (color and shading) and Krista Goll (modeling), *digital*

Don Shank,
digital

the Fireplace

FIERY ETM
555-4650

COAL 555-4650 ETM

Shank
8-24-2021
8-25-2021
8-26-2021

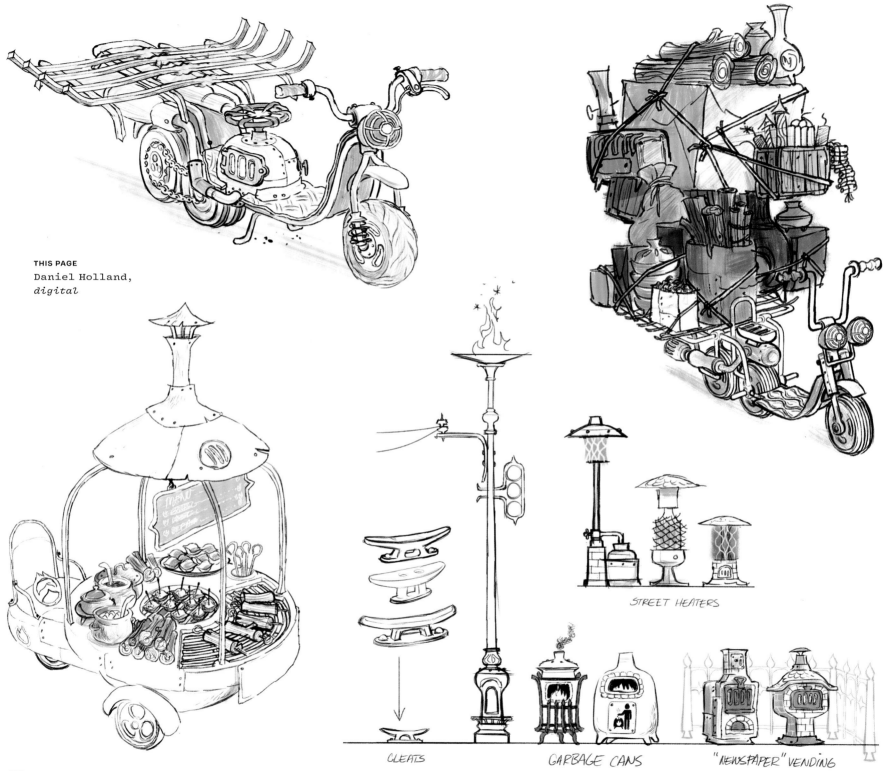

CLEATS

GARBAGE CANS

STREET HEATERS

"NEWSPAPER" VENDING

THE FIREPLACE

WOOD SNACKS · LAVA JAVA · KOL-NUTS

TOP Jasmine Cisneros, Lorraine Fitzgerald, Krista Goll, Jeanette Vera, Jane Wang, Raymond Wong (modeling); Tracy Church, Rich Snyder, Lan Tang, Andy Whittock (shading); Ben Von Zastrow (dressing); and Laura Meyer (graphics); *digital*

ABOVE Laura Meyer, *digital*

RIGHT Christian Roman, *digital*

We wanted Firetown to feel authentic. Fire built this town by themselves, so everything they built should feel like it has its own stories, cultures, and characteristics. We wanted to have reasons for everything we designed for this town, including sidewalks, signs, and windows.

Maria Yi, Characters Art Director

Maria Yi, *digital*

Maria Yi

Bernie is the heart of the film. He is the reason Ember wants to run the shop, and he is the emotional stake of the film. Like my father, he traveled a long distance, leaving his home to create a new life for his children. Part of the emotion for me was seeing how hard my father worked to make that dream a reality for our family. A challenge of Bernie's design was to see if we could capture that feel of a hardworking immigrant, but in fire—creating a character that used to have that strength to build up a shop, but now is aging and needing to retire. And then we had fun trying to capture the visual of a dying campfire to feel like a tired old dad.

Peter Sohn, Director

EATING GROWS him back.

Peter Sohn, *ink on paper*

Alice Lemma, *digital*

Jeeyoon Park, *digital*

Alice Lemma, *digital*

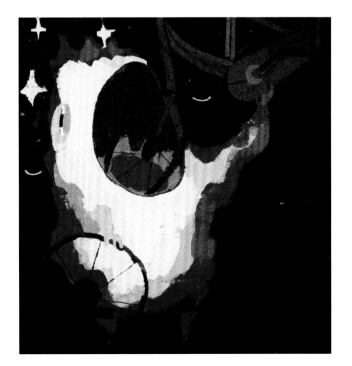

BOTTOM ROW Alice Lemma, *digital*

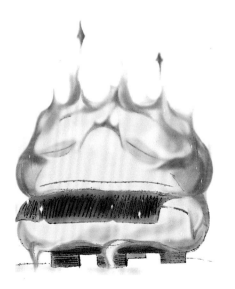

THIS SPREAD
Alice Lemma,
digital

Anna Benedict, *watercolor*

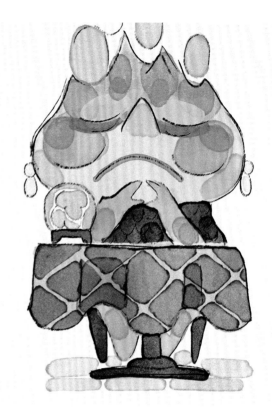

sparks in her eyes?
rose sparks?

leads with her nose
nose gets bigger

fast / on the hunt

pleasently
smelling

discovers a smell!

Cinder was an entertaining character to work on as it involved a lot of channeling that fun, overbearingly loving, mom/aunty figure that a lot of families can relate to.

Hyein Park, Story Artist

ABOVE, LEFT AND OPPOSITE
Alice Lemma, *digital*

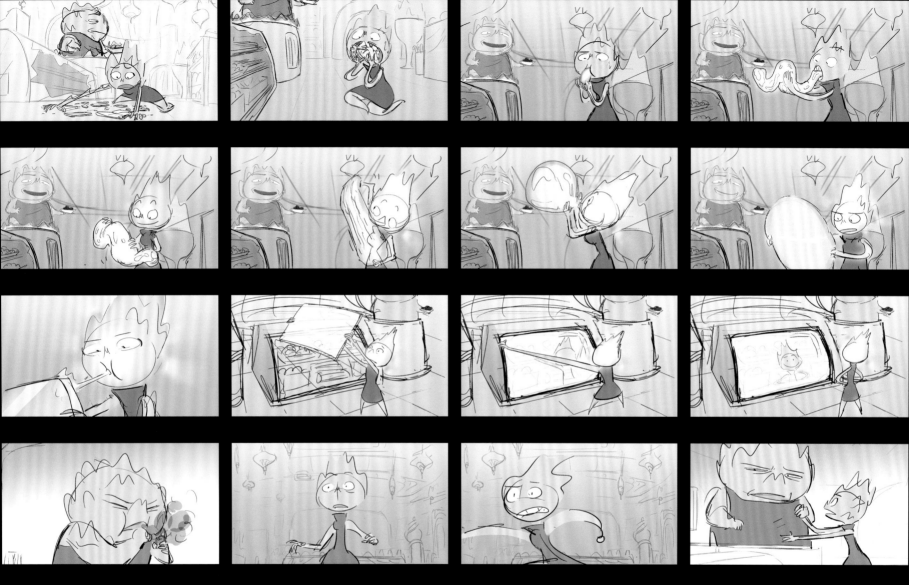

WHEN YOU ARE READY

Anna Benedict, Yung-Han Chang,
and Le Tang, *digital*

In this scene, we find Ember ten years after her vow to take over the shop—a promise
not yet fulfilled on account of her explosive temper. As she tries to fix her mistakes,
she's reminded of her father's growing inability to run the shop. This was a difficult
scene to board, as we wanted to fit in as much as we could about the state of Ember's
world in a short amount of time. From juggling performances with flaming iron bars to
mismatched suitors to annoying Water bros, the scene went through much transformation
before settling into this simple truth: Though she has small victories, Ember is still
not where she wants to be.

Anna Benedict, Story Artist

Alice Lemma and
Maria Yi, *digital*

Don Shank, *ink and watercolor on paper*

Maria Yi, *digital*

Don Shank, *digital*

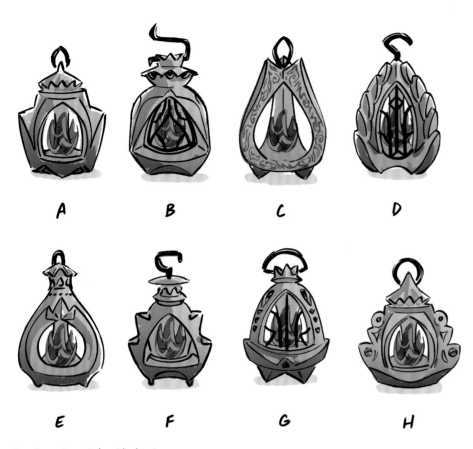

A B C D

E F G H

Meghan Sasaki, *digital*

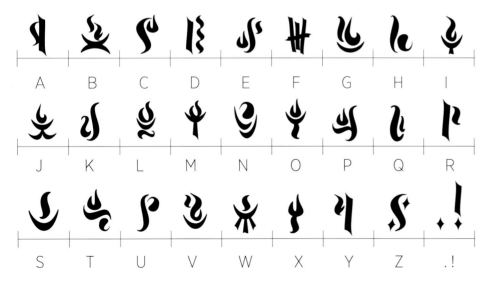

A	B	C	D	E	F	G	H	I

J	K	L	M	N	O	P	Q	R

S	T	U	V	W	X	Y	Z	.!

Laura Meyer, *digital*

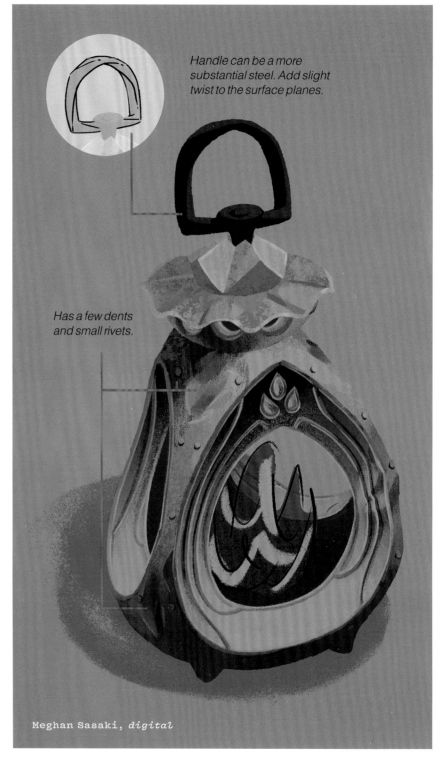

Handle can be a more substantial steel. Add slight twist to the surface planes.

Has a few dents and small rivets.

Meghan Sasaki, *digital*

Alice Lemma,
digital

Peter Sohn,
ink on paper

KEEP ETERNAL
Flame
higher

The Blue Flame is sacred to Bernie. Its
eternal light embodies the beliefs of his
culture—what it means to be Fire. Holding
on to the Flame means holding on to who
he is. But also for Bernie, the Flame is a
connection to where he came from—a reminder
of a life he loved, of places he cherished,
of family he so dearly misses.

Le Tang, Story Lead

ABOVE Yung-Han Chang, *digital*

Carlos Felipe León, *digital*

Daniel Holland,
digital

74

EMBER'S BEDROOM,
ANA'S EXPLORATION FOR REFERENCE

LOG PILLOW.

WORKAHOLIC

COALS.

LOG PILE

FIRE PLACE MANTLE FOR HEAD BOARD

WATER TRAIN OUTSIDE WINDOW

LOG PILLOW GETS EATEN BY FIRE

SOFA GRATE

GLOVE TO PUT TAPE INTO VCR.

VIDEO TAPES OF FIRELAND SOAP OPERAS

TECHNOLOGY HAVE NOT MOVED FROM 70'S-80'S

MOM CUTTING "APPLES"

PINE CONES (WOOD CHIPS)

Peter Sohn,
ink on paper

Meghan Sasaki,
digital

AIRFLOW

Daniel Holland, *digital*

Carlos Felipe León, *digital*

You Splash it You Buy it

🔥 Please 🔥
SCORCH YOURSELF

ABOVE AND BELOW
Laura Meyer, *digital*

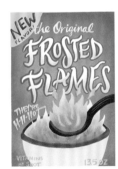

MENU

		SPECIAL
KOL-NUTS 5	WOOD PATTIES ... 2/5	CHARCOAL
HOT LOGS 8	HOT CHARROS ... 7	BRICK
WOOD CHIPS ... 6		MEAL
MATCH STIX SNACKS ... 7	SAP GLAZE ... 3	12

Fresh Molten **LAVA JAVA**

HOT **KOL-NUTS**

Laura Meyer, *digital*

FUEL UP!

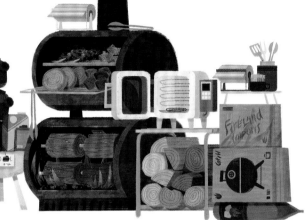

Lauren Kawahara, *digital*

Daniel Holland and
Lauren Kawahara (props), *digital*

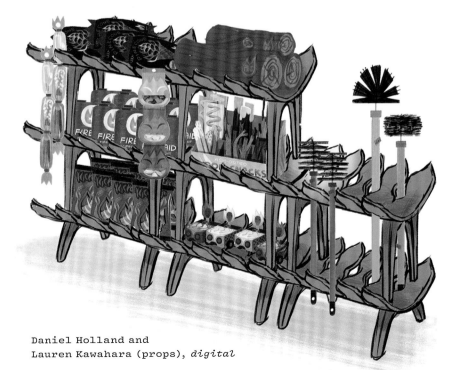

Daniel Holland and
Lauren Kawahara (props), *digital*

THIS SPREAD
Lauren Kawahara, *digital*

FIRE AID
FIRESTARTER KIT

Scorching Bubbles

FLAME-O
PRO-STRENGTH

Wick-ex

BURN OFF
HEAVY DUTY

Scorchgard
HEAVY DUTY
H_2O SHIELD

Bonfire

Smoky Haze

Hearth

METHANOL
EXTRA STRENGTH
Fever Enhancer

ASH-ORTED
WOOD SNACKS

SMOKE PUFFS

SIZZLIN'
SPARK
BARK

HEARTHY SOOT

SPARKLING KEROSENE

ETHANOL
FIZZ

DR. DIESEL

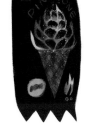

PINECONE

SPARKBURST

SPARK JOY

magmacard

SuperLight-O

TWIG

Pay

SPARK BALL

GLASS BLOWING CLASS!

STRIKER
Scorch

BURN OINTMENT

COMMUNITY BONFIRE!
8pm

Meghan Sasaki, *digital*

Lauren Kawahara (color and shading)
and Daniel Holland (design), *digital*

TAKE BREATH, MAKE CONNECTION Anna Benedict, Jason Katz, Dan Park, and Jeeyoon Park, *digital*

Peter Sohn, *digital*

everyone
sits
on
floor.

1 foot
Raised.

ANCIENT
MARKINGS.

Peter Sohn,
ink on paper

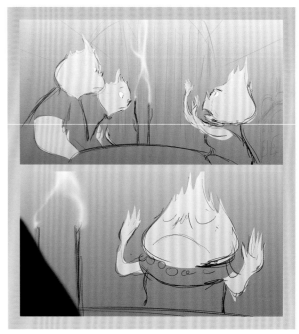

Le Tang, *digital*

Meghan Sasaki, *digital*

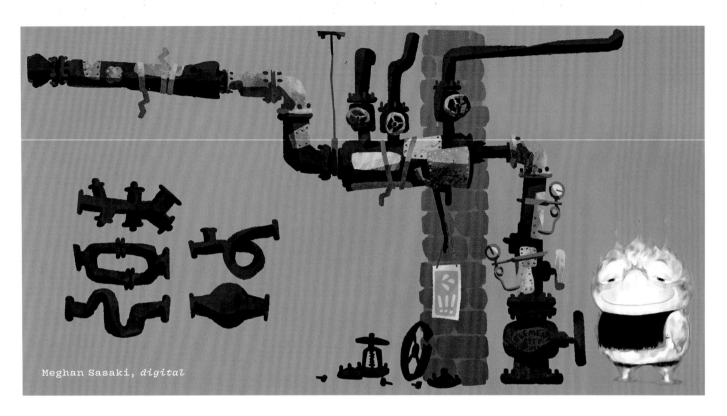

Meghan Sasaki, *digital*

Jasmine Cisneros (dressing), Clara Prado Vazquez (modeling), and Rui Tong (shading); *digital*

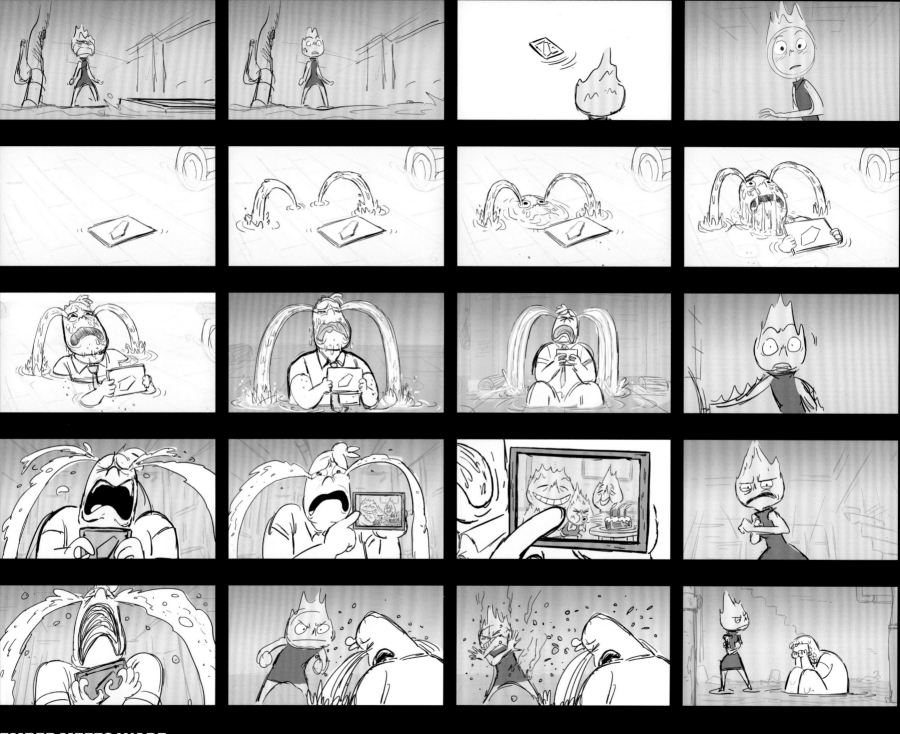

EMBER MEETS WADE Anna Benedict, Yung-Han Chang, Nira Liu, Austin Madison, Peter Sohn, and Le Tang, *digital*

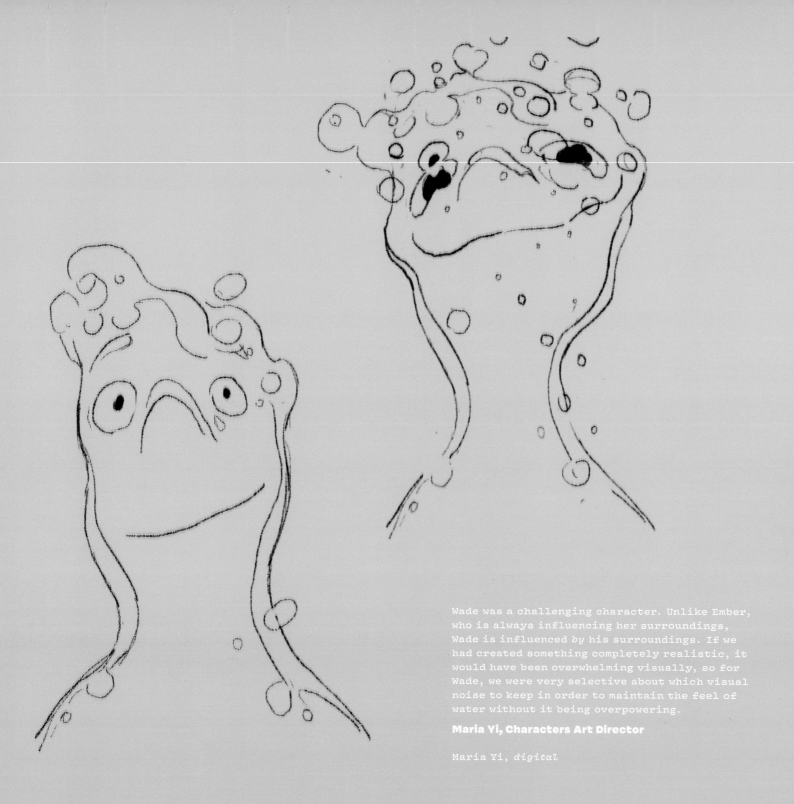

Wade was a challenging character. Unlike Ember, who is always influencing her surroundings, Wade is influenced *by* his surroundings. If we had created something completely realistic, it would have been overwhelming visually, so for Wade, we were very selective about which visual noise to keep in order to maintain the feel of water without it being overpowering.

Maria Yi, Characters Art Director

Maria Yi, *digital*

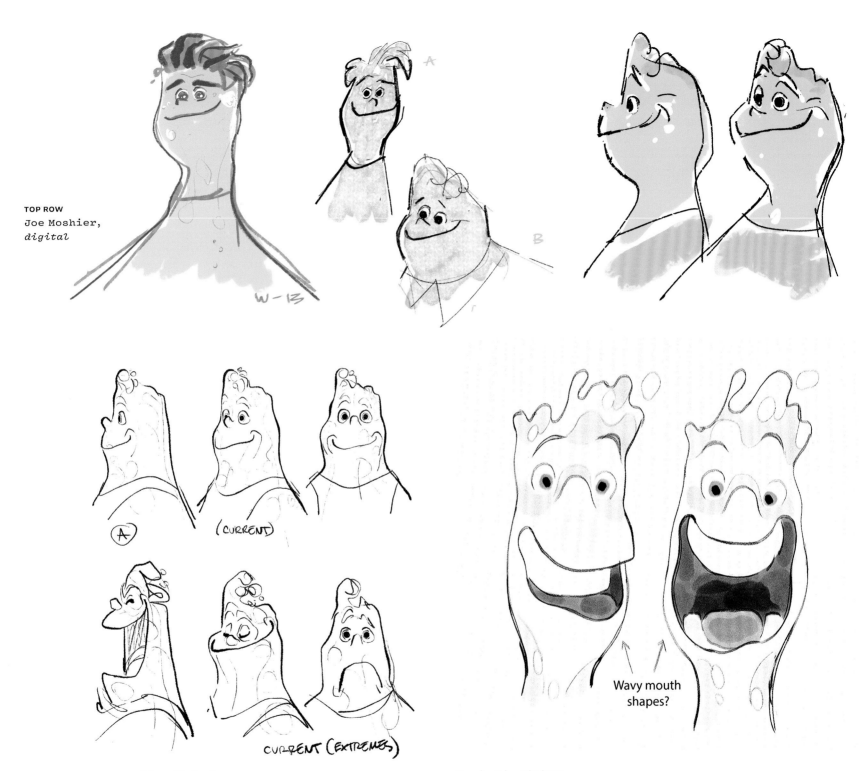

W-13

Ⓐ

(CURRENT)

CURRENT (EXTREMES)

Wavy mouth
shapes?

Tony Fucile, *digital*

Maria Yi, *digital*

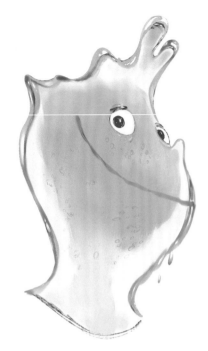

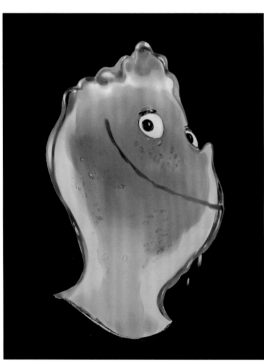

Daniel López Muñoz, *pencil and digital*

Anatomy of Lumen Water

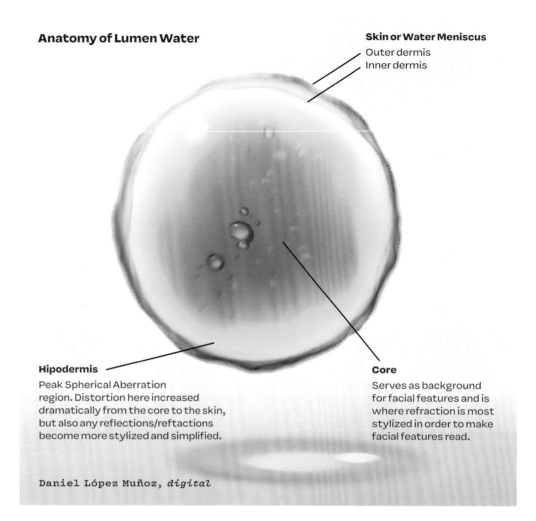

Skin or Water Meniscus
Outer dermis
Inner dermis

Hipodermis
Peak Spherical Aberration region. Distortion here increased dramatically from the core to the skin, but also any reflections/reftactions become more stylized and simplified.

Core
Serves as background for facial features and is where refraction is most stylized in order to make facial features read.

Daniel López Muñoz, *digital*

Like Ember, we prioritized Wade's personality first and foremost in the design. Reflections and refraction of real water would play second fiddle and were only used to support believability of the element. We also wanted a bold gesture to the character's outline, opting to use the nature of the element to do the expressive job of linework. Based on an early painting of Wade's head that caught Pete's eye, we settled that it should look like the meniscus curve you see when water presses up against the inner walls of a glass to delineate Wade's "dermis." The test I devised for this was a lot simpler than Ember's—also hand-painted, frame by frame. A water sphere gently undulating in the air was enough to convey the attributes we wanted for the look of Wade's water. For his inner core, we distorted the background enough to bring across his facial features with greater clarity.

Daniel López Muñoz, Concept Designer

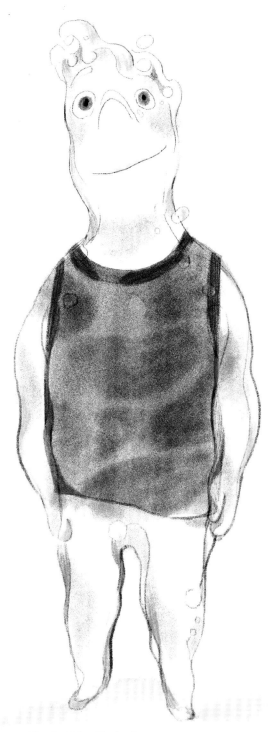

Maria Yi, *digital*

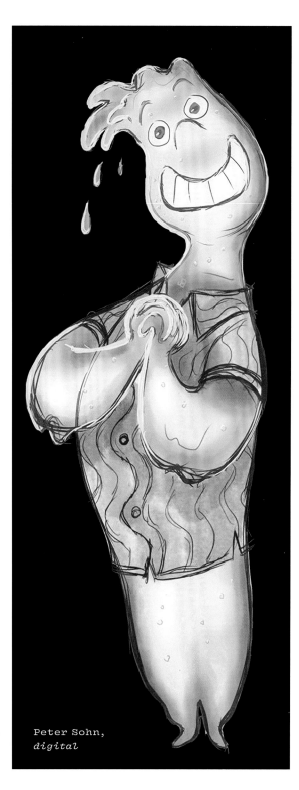

Peter Sohn,
digital

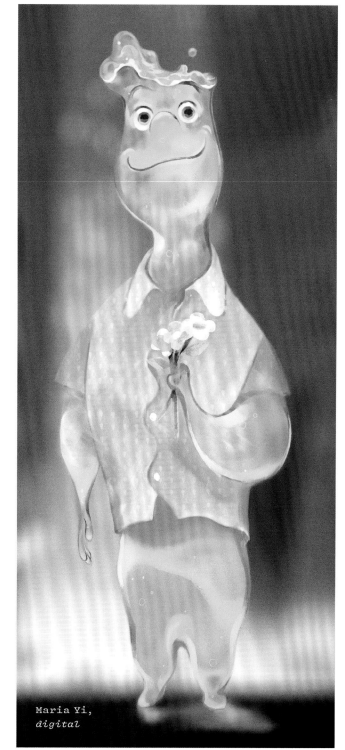

Maria Yi,
digital

Maria Yi,
digital

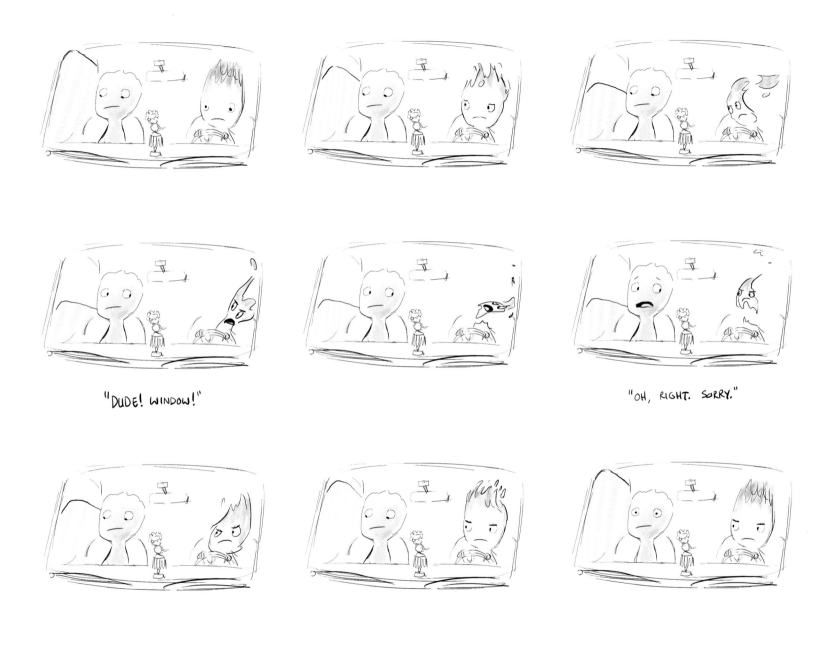

"DUDE! WINDOW!"   "OH, RIGHT. SORRY."

Austin Madison, *digital*

THE WETRO

Peter Sohn,
ink on paper

Nat McLaughlin,
digital

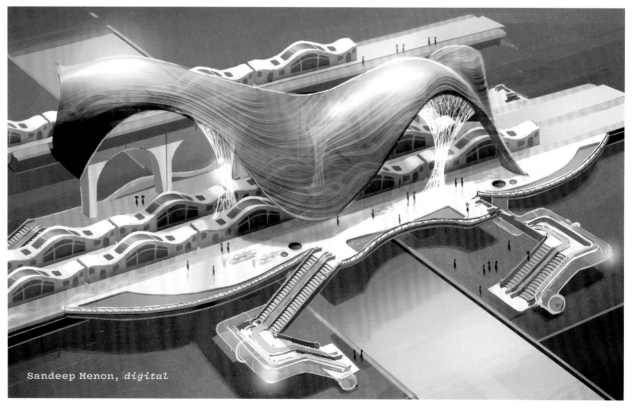

Sandeep Menon, *digital*

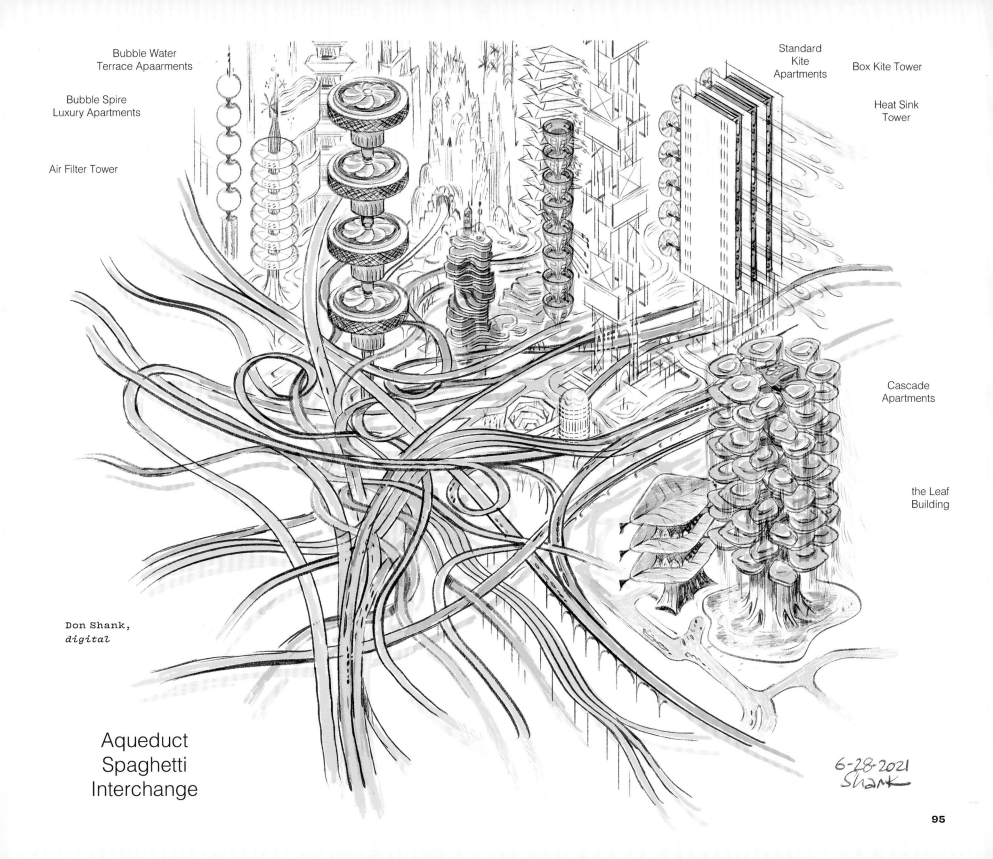

Bubble Water
Terrace Apaarments

Bubble Spire
Luxury Apartments

Air Filter Tower

Standard
Kite
Apartments

Box Kite Tower

Heat Sink
Tower

Cascade
Apartments

the Leaf
Building

Don Shank,
digital

Aqueduct
Spaghetti
Interchange

6-28-2021
Shank

Nat McLaughlin, *digital*

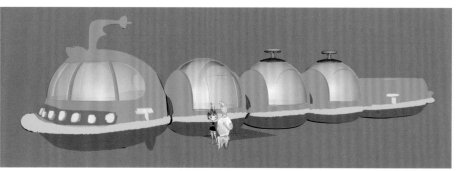

ABOVE Lauren Kawahara
(color design) and Jeanette
Vera (modeling), *digital*

LEFT Nat McLaughlin, *digital*

headlights

wavy decals

drain plates

For the vehicles, I started with Don's amazing
drawings of Element City and tried to imagine what
would feel right in there, breaking them down by
element type and purpose. Submarines? Cars? Drivable
trees? Everything was thrown into the mix in a great
brainstorm to help Pete achieve his vision.

Nat McLaughlin, Environments Designer

Peter Sohn, *digital*

Le Tang, *digital*

EARTH

Alice Lemma,
digital

Zaruhi Galstyan, *digital*

Daniel Holland, *ink and watercolor on paper*

Daniel Holland,
ink and watercolor on paper

TOP ROW AND ABOVE Daniel Holland, *digital*

Daniel Holland, *ink and watercolor on paper*

THIS PAGE
Alice Lemma, *digital*

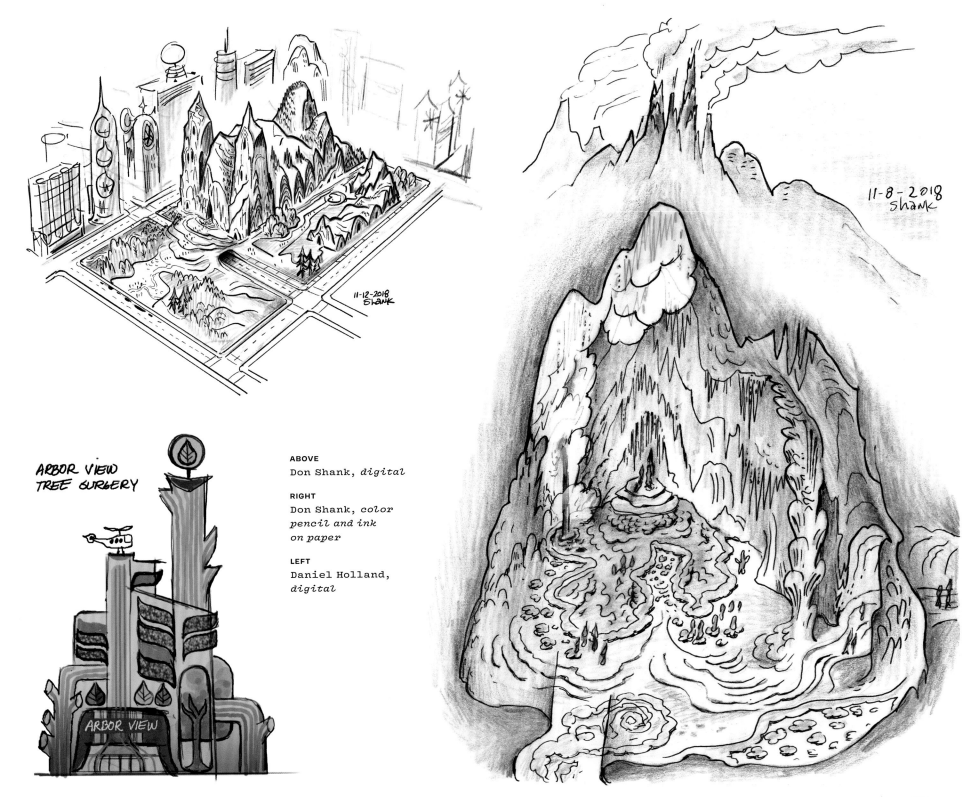

ARBOR VIEW
TREE SURGERY

ABOVE
Don Shank, *digital*

RIGHT
Don Shank, *color pencil and ink on paper*

LEFT
Daniel Holland, *digital*

These building designs represent the idea that characters in Element City are all living together. There is fun and richness in having both Water and Earth characters living in the same building and neighborhood. I was also trying to think logically about how Water characters might live higher up to allow for water to trickle down and water the Earth characters.

Daniel Holland, Environments Art Director

THIS SPREAD Daniel Holland,
ink and watercolor on paper

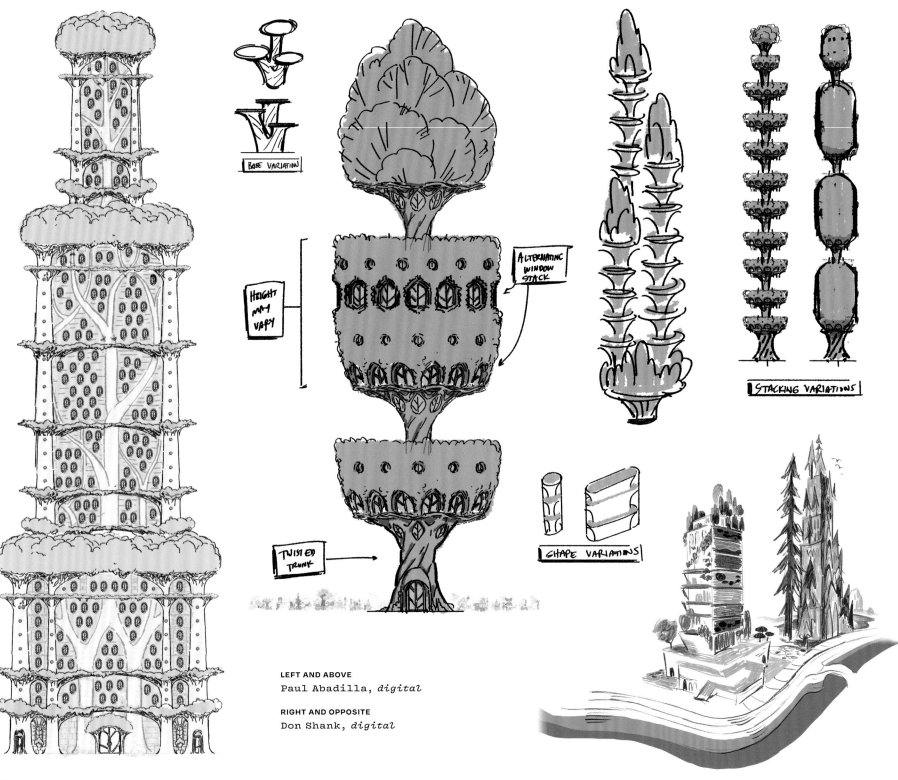

BASE VARIATION

ALTERNATING WINDOW STACK

HEIGHT MAY VARY

TWISTED TRUNK

STACKING VARIATIONS

SHAPE VARIATIONS

LEFT AND ABOVE
Paul Abadilla, *digital*

RIGHT AND OPPOSITE
Don Shank, *digital*

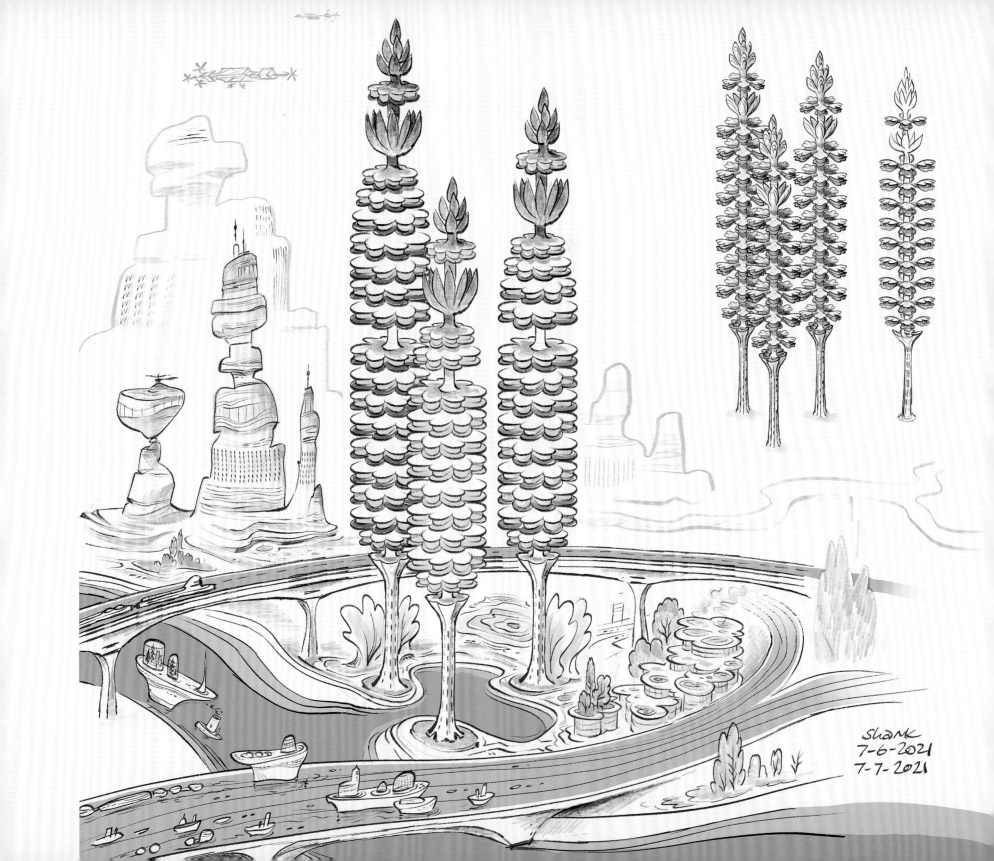

THIS PAGE Zaruhi Galstyan, *collage*

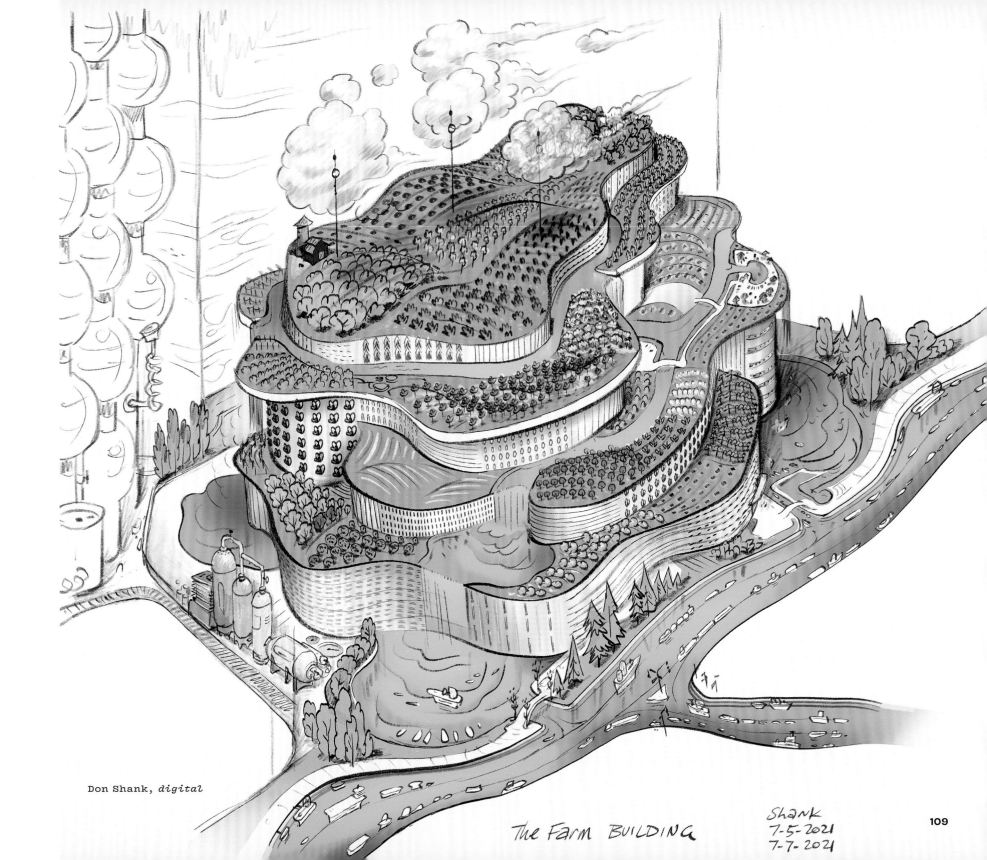

Don Shank, *digital*

The Farm Building

Shank
7-5-2021
7-7-2021

Nat McLaughlin, *digital*

THIS PAGE Anna Scott, *digital*

111

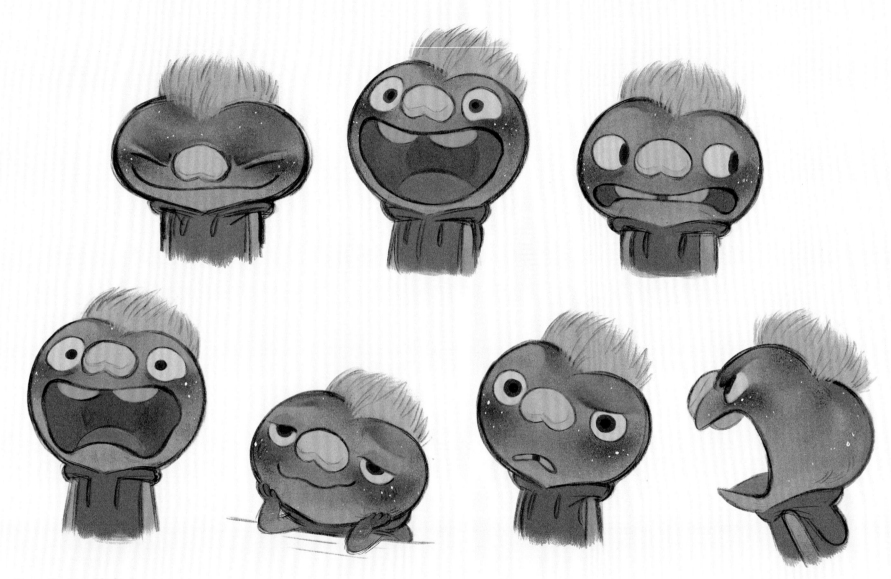

Anna Scott, *digital*

112

Carlos Felipe León, *digital*

Yung-Han Chang and Peter Sohn, *digital*

When designing the Clod character, one of the key parts to his identity is his crush on Ember. We thought it would be fitting to reflect that side of him by giving him a heart-shaped head and nose.

Anna Scott, Character Designer

Anna Scott, *digital*

THIS PAGE Daniel López Muñoz, *digital*

OPPOSITE Lauren Kawahara (color and shading),
Daniel López Muñoz (set design), and Maria Yi (character design); *digital*

likes to play tetris

Fern was a really fun character to design. He is a "done with life" bureaucrat who spends his life at work. So much so that his vegetation has overgrown to take over his whole office, and he has become one with it. He was the first Earth character we designed, so through him we started exploring the look of dirt and foliage for the movie, which was an exciting challenge. In these early sketches I was trying to capture his personality, figuring out what kind of plants might grow on him and what their leaves could look like.

**Alice Lemma,
Character Designer**

FORM
2C1A

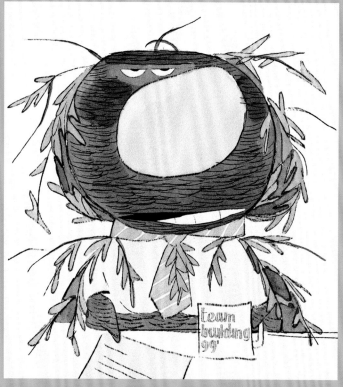

team building 99'

THIS SPREAD
Alice Lemma,
digital

Alice Lemma (character)
and Nat McLaughlin, *digital*

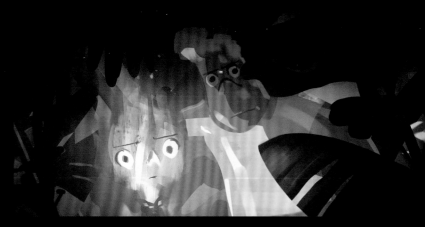

Daniel Holland, *ink and watercolor on paper*

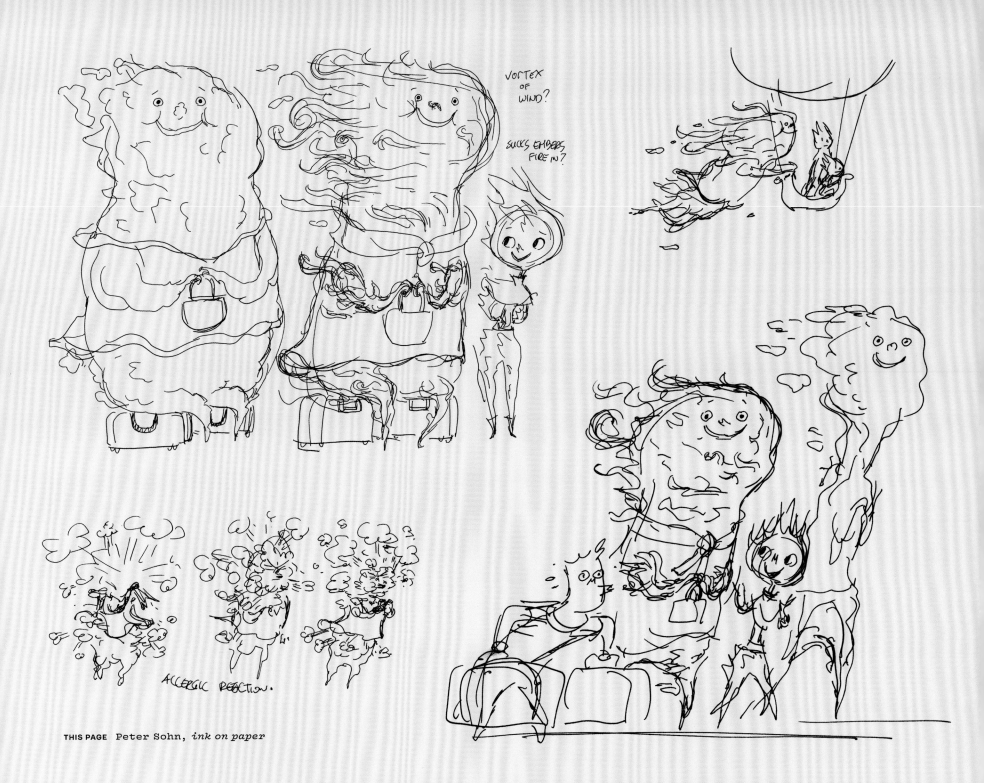

VORTEX OF WIND?

SUCKS EMBERS FIRE IN?

ALLERGIC REACTION.

When I first started working on *Elemental*,
I tried making an Air character out of cotton.
The end result didn't quite capture the wispy
quality that Air characters needed to have in
the movie, but it was still a very fun project.
Knitting his little scarf was my favorite part.

Alice Lemma, Character Designer

RIGHT Alice Lemma, *cotton and yarn*

Don Shank,
*color pencil
and ink on paper*

Alice Lemma, *digital*

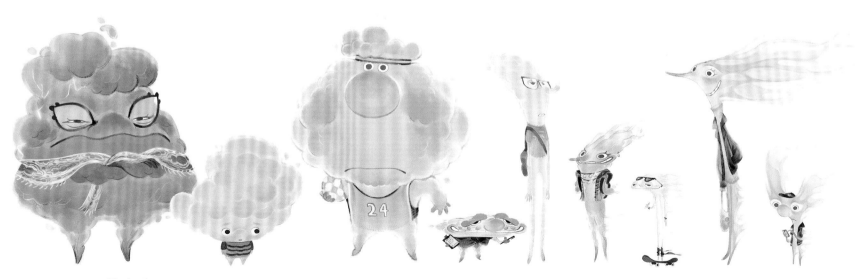

Anna Scott, *digital*

Bill Presing, *digital*

LEFT AND OPPOSITE
Maria Yi, *digital*

Don Shank,
*color pencil and
ink on paper*

The Air District is only seen in one sequence,
but it was still just as important to make it
feel as believable in Elemental culture as the
other districts. The stadium area is lively and
bustling, so besides looking for ways to "see
air" in the setting and architecture, we wanted
to layer a big city sports center filled with
visual fanfare and electricity.

Don Shank, Production Designer

CYCLONE
STADIUM

Jasmin Lai, *digital*

Daniel López Muñoz, *digital*

ABOVE Jennifer Chia-Han Chang,
Jack Hattori (color and shading);
and Nat McLaughlin (design); *digital*

LEFT Jennifer Chia-Han Chang,
Jack Hattori (color and shading);
and Maria Yi (characters); *digital*

BELOW Laura Meyer, *digital*

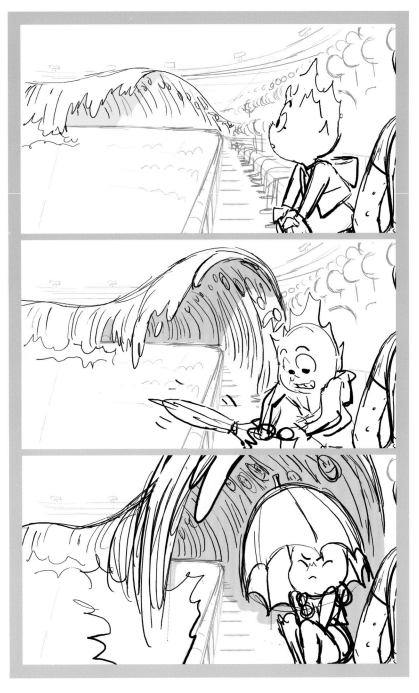

ABOVE Bill Presing, *digital*

LEFT Maria Yi, *digital*

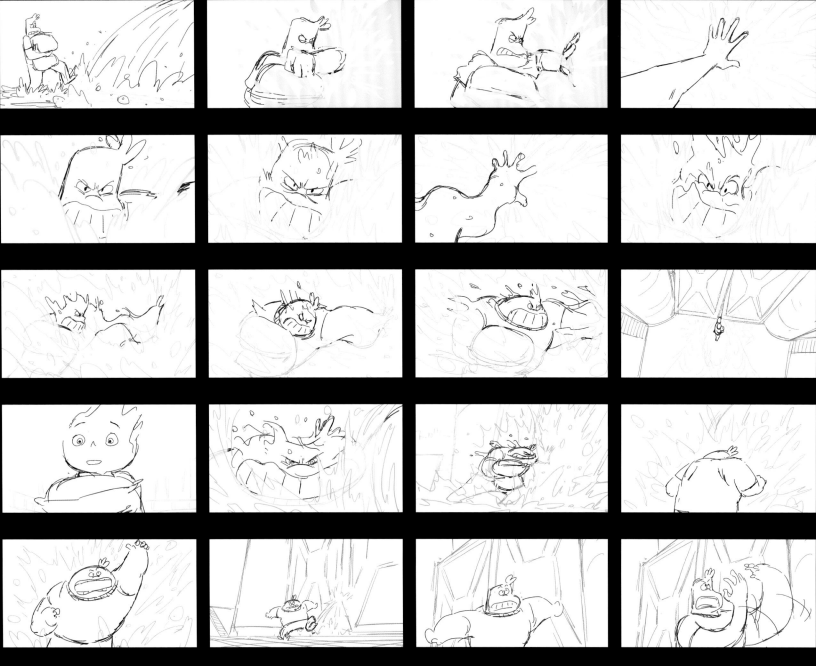

EMBER, THROW ME MORE SANDBAGS

Yung-Han Chang, *digital*

The goal of this moment is to show a different side of Wade's character.
Wade is willing to push himself and reach his limit in order to help Ember.
That endeavor is what changes Ember's opinion about Wade.

Yung-Han Chang, Story Artist

Jasmin Lai, *digital*

THIS PAGE Ralph Eggleston, *digital*

Daniel López Muñoz, *pencil, ink, and digital*

Kyle Macnaughton, *digital*

THIS SPREAD
Maria Yi, *digital*

"Ember! Ember! Over here!"

Daniel López Muñoz,
pencil and digital

THIS PAGE Carlos Felipe León, *digital*

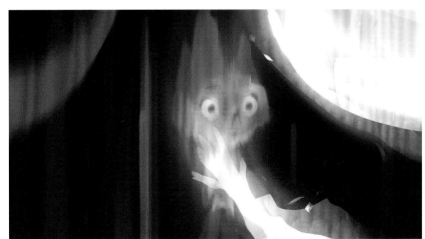

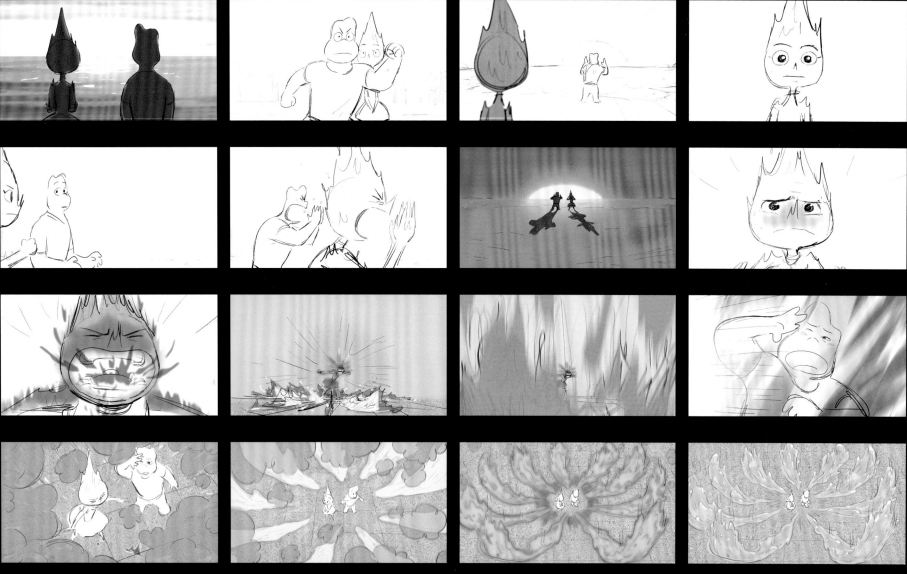

EMBER CREATES GLASS

Hyein Park, Jeeyoon Park
and Le Tang, *digital*

This scene, while it appears slightly different in the film than depicted in these boards,
comes directly from a personal experience I shared with Story Lead Le Tang. He was giving me
a ride to the train station one night and tried to get me to loosen up by having me scream as
loud as I could. To help, Le blasted the music on full, and also decided to scream incredibly
loud alongside me. In order to express the complex feelings and microemotions Ember feels
in this scene, I would consistently recall that time in Le's car, trying to capture that
genuine hesitancy of stepping outside of one's comfort zone, and the liberating feeling of
tearing down one's inner wall. For me, it was a night to remember in that car, and hopefully,
that same special feeling is passed on to the audience.

Jeeyoon Park, Story Artist

Peter Sohn, *digital*

WATER

TROUBLED WATERS MEDICAL CENTER

Daniel Holland, *digital*

Alice Lemma, *digital*

Maria Yi, *digital*

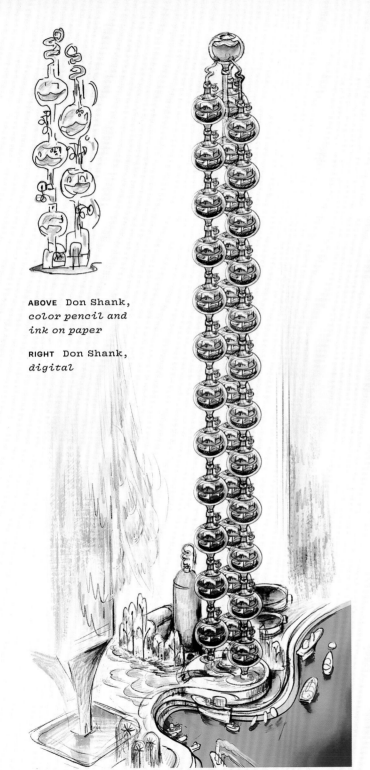

ABOVE Don Shank, *color pencil and ink on paper*

RIGHT Don Shank, *digital*

CLOUD GENERATOR

ROOFTOP LAKE

FALLS TURN TO MIST

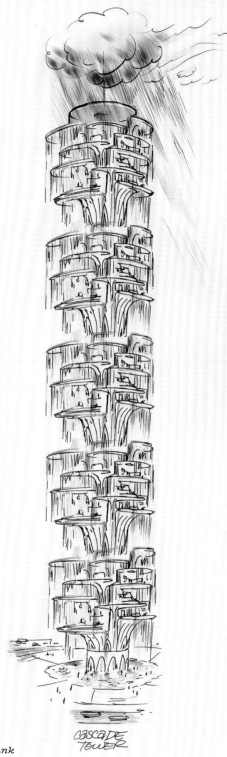

CASCADE TOWER

This apartment tower of cascading pools of water was a very early concept to look for a fun way to mix an elemental feature into an apartment skyscraper. When we needed a setting for Brook's apartment, this idea seemed perfectly suited. First, we adapted it to be a bit more regular and cylindrical. Then, in the modeling phase, the design was pushed even further to match what was already designed and built for her apartment interior.

Don Shank, Production Designer

ABOVE Don Shank, *color pencil and ink on paper*

RIGHT Don Shank, *digital over color pencil and ink*

TOP ROW AND BELOW
Don Shank, *color pencil and ink on paper*

LIGHTNING
RAIN CLOUDS

Shank
10-31-2018

Shank

the VASE BUILDING

HALF FULL APTS.

the WAVE BUILDING

DOWN

Shank
6-29-2021

Don Shank, *digital over pencil and color pencil*

Don Shank, *digital*

Jasmin Lai, *digital*

SHANK
11-2-2018

DAM
BUILDING
TOP

ROOFTOP
AQUARIUM
BALLROOM

Don Shank, *color pencil
and ink on paper*

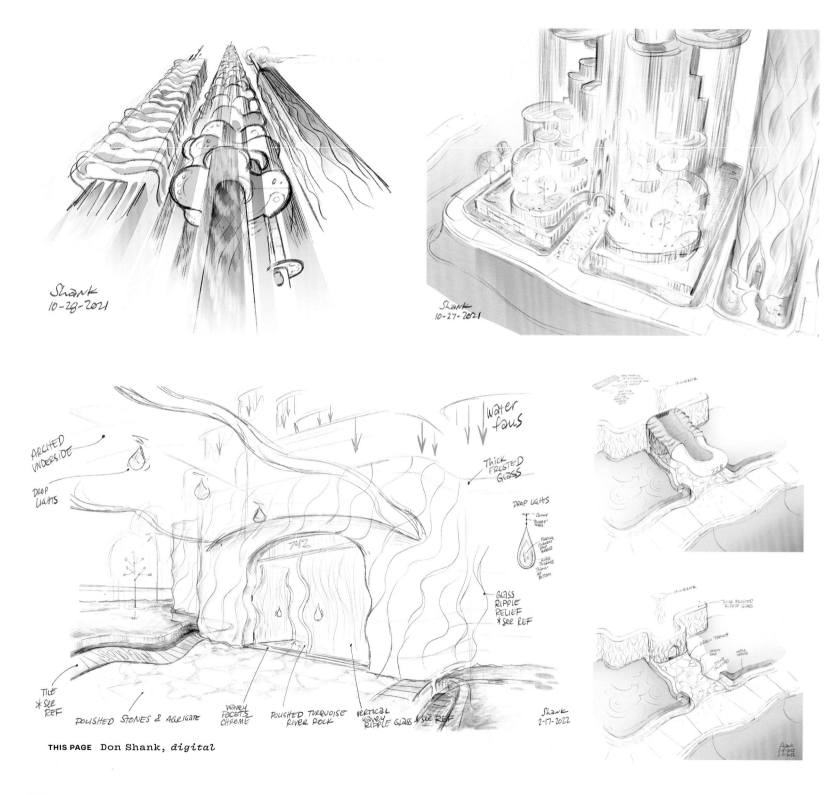

Shank
10-28-2021

Shank
10-27-2021

ARCHED
UNDERSIDE

DROP
LIGHTS

water
fans

Thick
Frosted
Glass

DROP LIGHTS

GLASS
RIPPLE
RELIEF
✷ SEE REF

TILE
✷ SEE
REF

POLISHED STONES & AGRIGATE

WAVEY
FACETS
CHROME

POLISHED TURQUOISE
RIVER ROCK

VERTICAL
WAVEY
RIPPLE GLASS ✷ SEE REF

Shank
2-17-2022

THIS PAGE Don Shank, *digital*

148

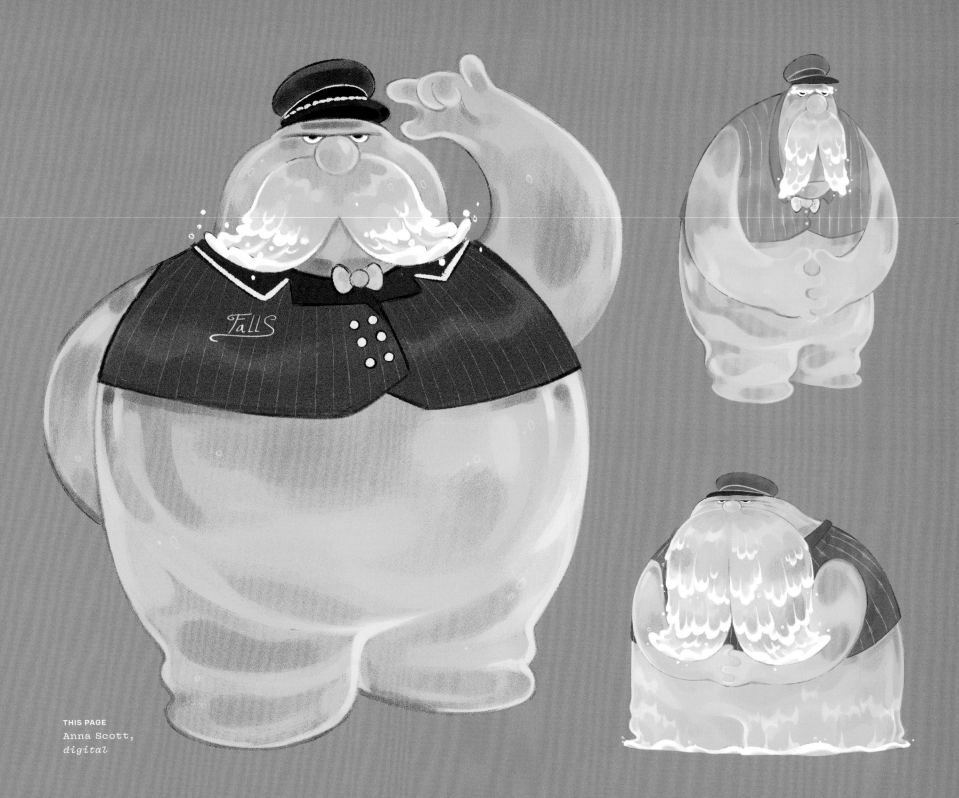

149

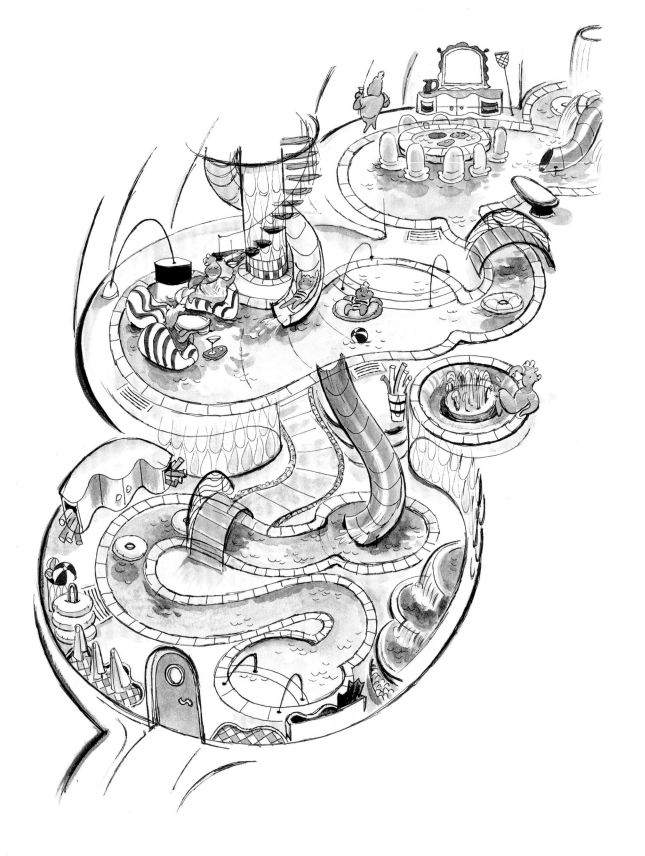

The design of the Water apartment is reminiscent of a water park, where every room is a different pool with fun water features and full of pool-related objects. We imagined that instead of hallways, the Ripples could float between rooms down a lazy river, which was in part inspired by Disney's Aulani resort. At the same time, this space feels like a modern art museum, reflecting Brook's high-end taste and work. It's a funny mix of high art and cheap inflatable furniture.

Daniela Strijleva, Environments Designer

LEFT Daniela Strijleva,
ink and watercolor on paper

ABOVE Daniela Strijleva,
marker and digital color

Daniela Strijleva, *marker and digital color*

Carlos Felipe León, *digital*

Daniela Strijleva, *marker and digital color*

Daniela Strijleva, *digital*

Daniela Strijleva, *digital*

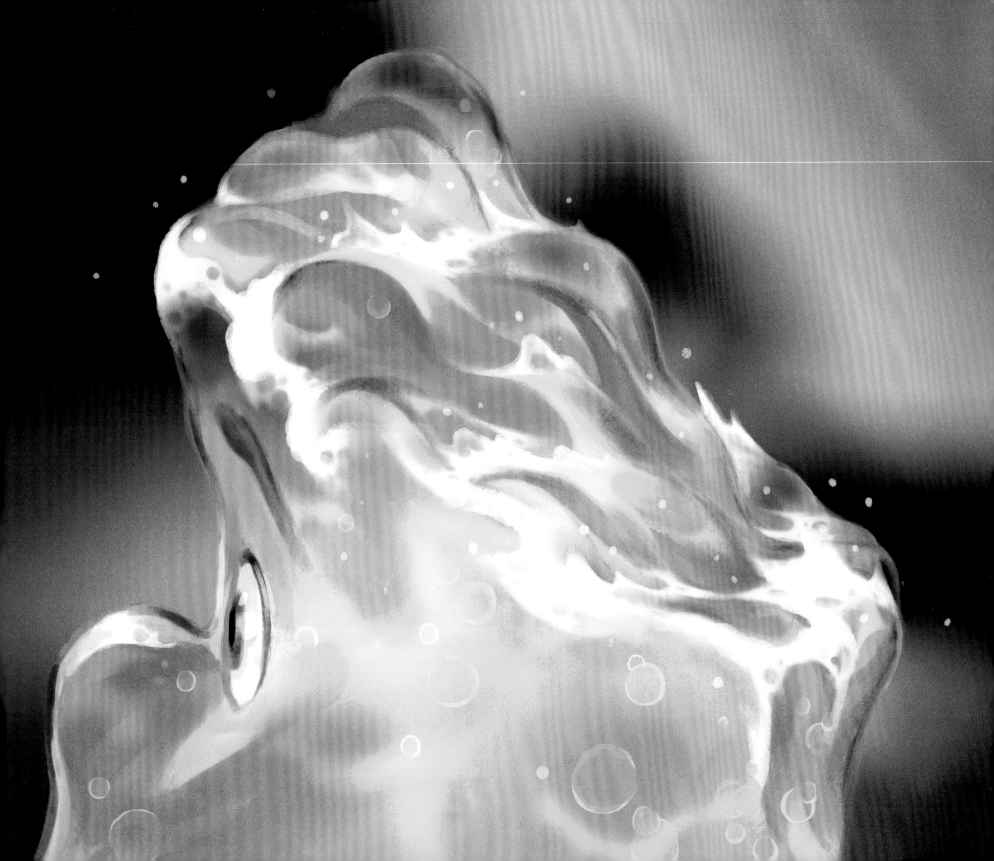

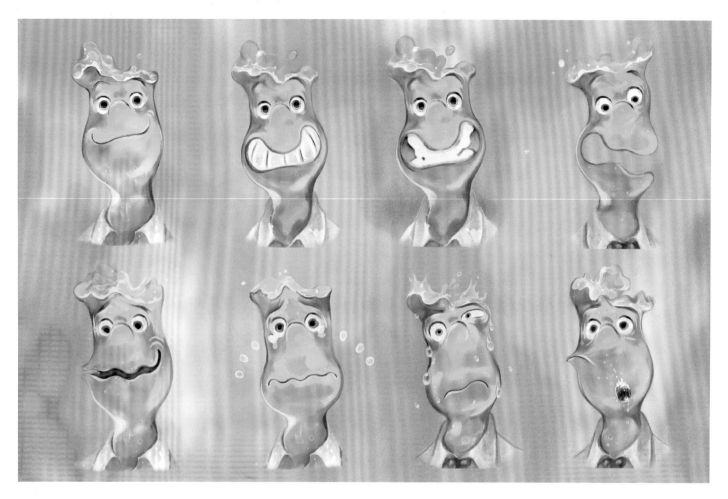

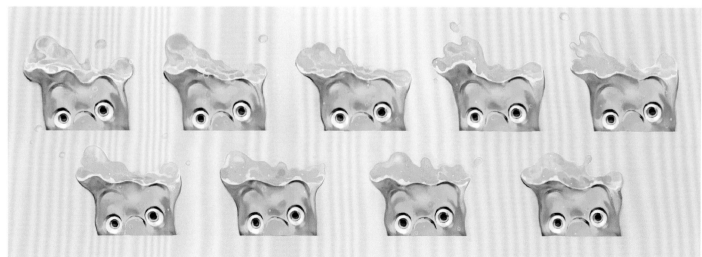

THIS SPREAD
Maria Yi, *digital*

"Hey, do you like my hair splashed-back?"

"That sounds so stupid. Urghhhhh!"

THIS SPREAD
Maria Yi, *digital*

"I GOTTA LEVEL OUT"

Don Shank,
ink on paper

Anna Scott,
digital

Maria Yi,
digital

OCEAN FAMILY

RIVER FAMILY

THIS PAGE
Peter Sohn,
digital

THIS PAGE
Alice Lemma,
digital

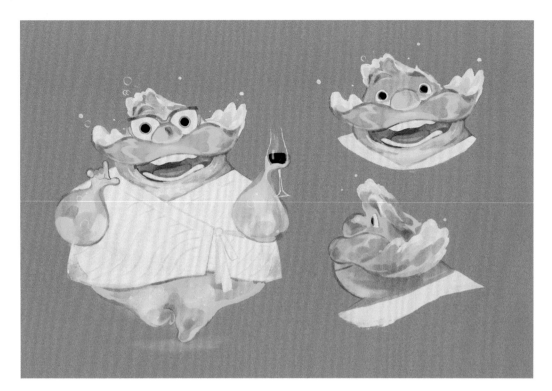

THIS PAGE
Maria Yi,
digital

161

THIS SPREAD
Anna Scott,
digital

Josh West, *digital*

We needed something iconic from above, a building that could be memorable by its shape and tie it to the Earth elements when Ember sees it from high up. There are two points in the film where we would see Garden Central Station, and our hope was that once you saw it, you would remember it for later.

Peter Sohn, *Director*

OPPOSITE
Anna Scott, *digital*

THIS PAGE
Daniel López Muñoz, *digital*

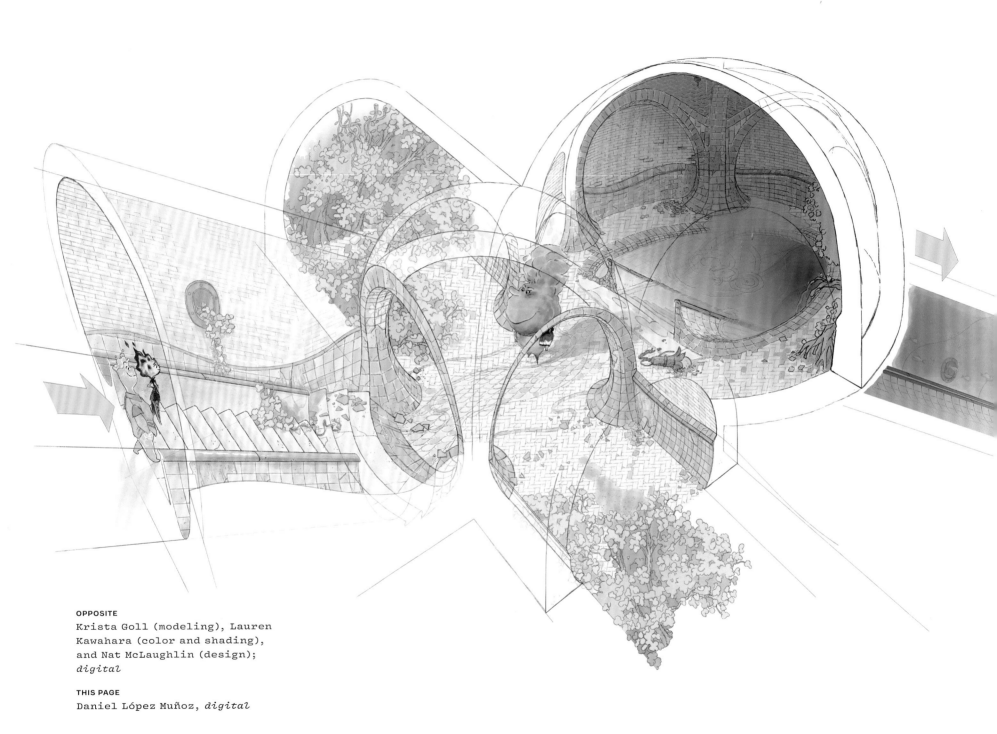

OPPOSITE
Krista Goll (modeling), Lauren
Kawahara (color and shading),
and Nat McLaughlin (design);
digital

THIS PAGE
Daniel López Muñoz, *digital*

Meghan Sasaki, *digital*

Nat McLaughlin, *digital*

Kyle Macnaughton, *digital over ink and marker*

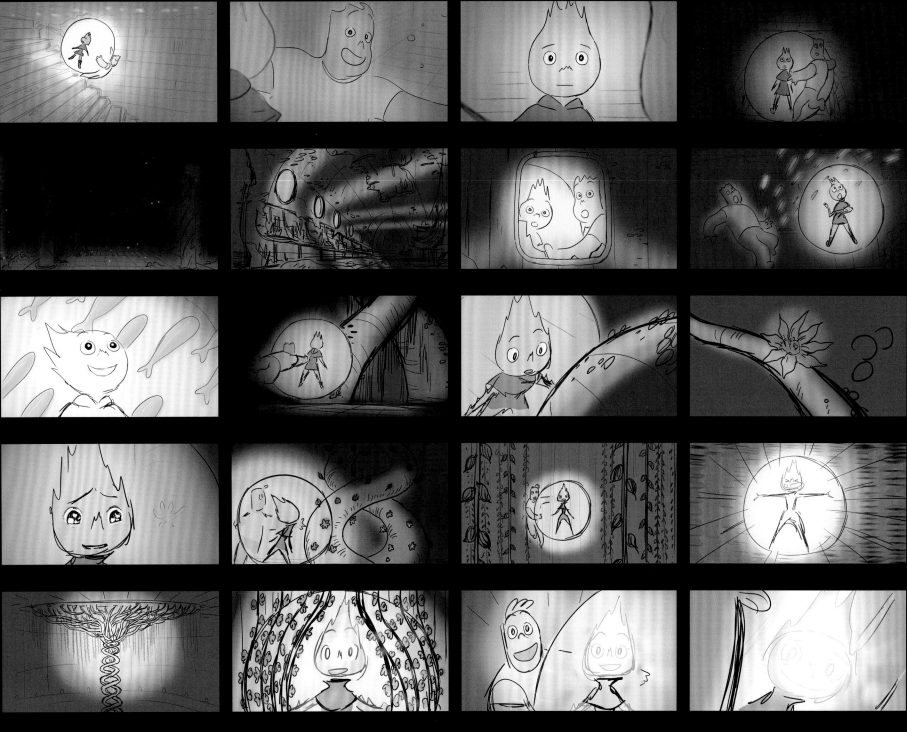

BUBBLE DATE Jason Katz, Nira Liu, and Le Tang, *digital*

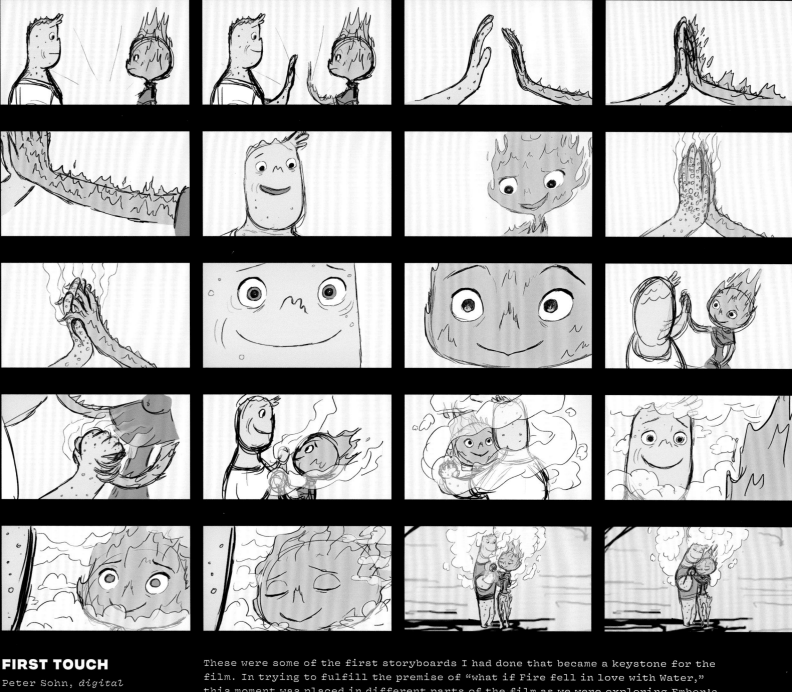

FIRST TOUCH
Peter Sohn, *digital*

These were some of the first storyboards I had done that became a keystone for the film. In trying to fulfill the premise of "what if Fire fell in love with Water," this moment was placed in different parts of the film as we were exploring Ember's journey. The moment being when Ember and Wade finally connect and wonder if it was even possible for them—a high point for Ember and her place in Element City.

Peter Sohn, Director

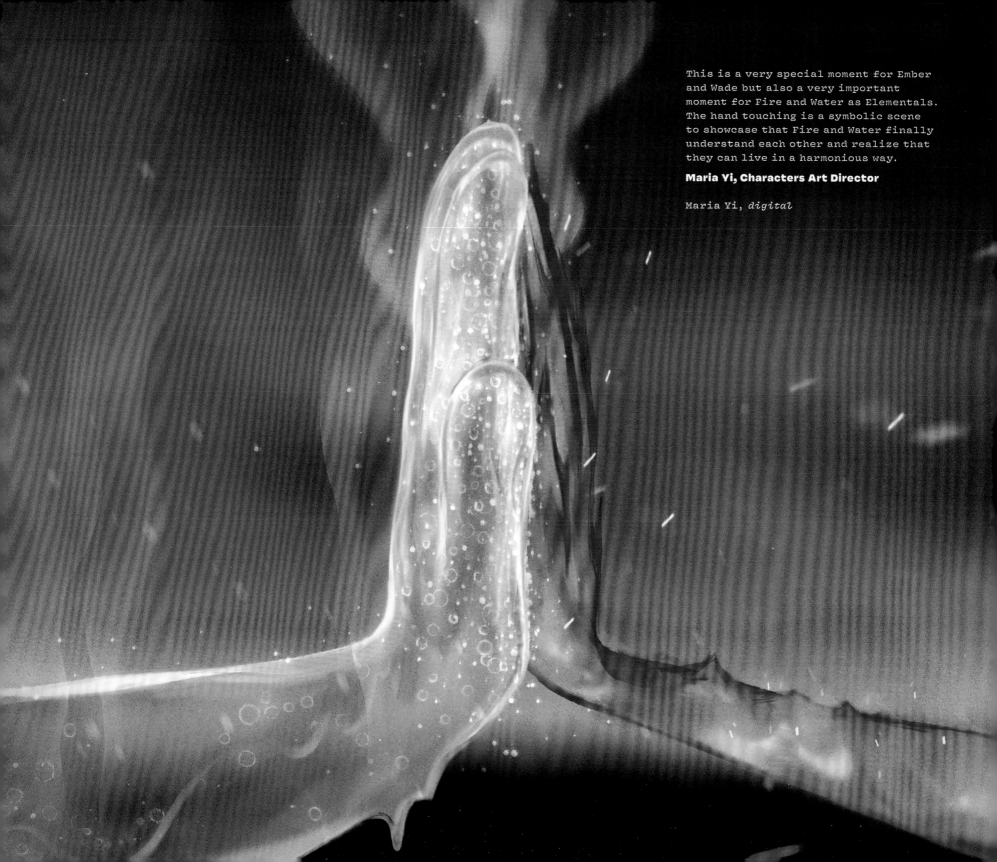

This is a very special moment for Ember and Wade but also a very important moment for Fire and Water as Elementals. The hand touching is a symbolic scene to showcase that Fire and Water finally understand each other and realize that they can live in a harmonious way.

Maria Yi, Characters Art Director

Maria Yi, *digital*

Acknowledgments

No one worked harder on *Elemental* than Pete Sohn. With his unparalleled passion and vision, Pete has shared his very personal and heartfelt family story with the world, and we are all the better for it. What resonates the most for me about this story is how it highlights the tremendous sacrifices parents make to fulfill the universal dream of giving their children a better life. I am profoundly grateful to Pete for the gift of greater insight and a deeper appreciation for everything my father did for me.

Thank you to everyone at Pixar who shared their incredibly moving experiences being a first- or second-generation immigrant to the United States. You deeply influenced the film, and hearing your stories is truly one of the highlights of my time at Pixar.

Special thanks to Erika Schmidt, who enthusiastically researched the daunting subject of immigration with great curiosity and sensitivity. We are grateful to all of our consultants, whose insights and guidance were instrumental in setting us off on the right path as we developed the story: 1951 Coffee Company; Dr. Kevin Chun; The Crucible in Oakland, California; Steven Davison at Walt Disney Creative Entertainment; Shirley Gee; Evy Kavaler; Lauren Williams; and the Vietnamese American Community Center of the East Bay.

Story Supervisor Jason Katz is the wise man of Story. He thoughtfully led with patience and kindness, and the production is indebted to him for his savvy and experience. Thank you to Story Lead Le Tang, who can do anything and is on my MVP Hall of Fame list, and to the world's greatest story team, who showed up with optimism and creativity every single day, no matter how many sequences they had to redraw:

Anna Benedict, Bolhem Bouchiba, Yung-Han Chang, Koko Chou, Nira Liu, Austin Madison, Hyein Park, Jeeyoon Park, Bill Presing, Chris Roman, and Mike Wu.

Thank you to writer Brenda Hsueh, who really gave voice to Ember, and put so much of herself in that character; and to writers John Hoberg and Kat Likkel for their exceptional patience, grace, humor, and willingness to try any and every story suggestion thrown their way.

Elemental's Story Department production team members are not only hardworking, funny, and smart but also an integral part of our filmmaking process. Pixar is very lucky to have managers like Cara Brody, Claire Faggioli, Kat Hendrickson, Meredith Hom, and Max Sachar and coordinators like Jessica Amen and Jess Walley. We are fortunate to have worked with such talented colleagues.

Pete shares an artistic and aesthetic connection with our Production Designer Don Shank, which had an undeniable impact on the film. After a short stint in development, Don created the drawings that would become Pete's North Star for designing the world of *Elemental*. Don was joined by Art Directors Jennifer Chia-Han Chang, Daniel Holland, Laura Meyer, and Maria Yi, who rolled with unprecedented challenges and whose talent and leadership were truly something to behold. We appreciate all the artists who brought our characters and world to life: Paul Abadilla, Lauren Kawahara, Jasmin Lai, Alice Lemma, Carlos Felipe Léon, Daniel López Muñoz, Albert Lozano, Kyle Macnaughton, Nat McLaughlin, Philip Metschan, Hye Sung Park, Meghan Sasaki, Anna Scott, Daniela Strijleva, and Rachel Xin.

Thank you to managers Maureen Giblin, Daniella Muller, and Rebecca Euphrat Regan, as well as coordinators Sydney Johnson, Michelle Li, and Jasmine Williams. This resourceful Art Department production team worked through significant disruption and unforeseen challenges with poise, humility, and a collaborative spirit.

As someone who adores books, it's always a joy to work with the smart Pixar Publishing team and the folks at Chronicle Books, who share with me a deep love of words and art. Thank you to Becca Boe, Deborah Cichocki, Neil Egan, Liam Flanagan, Molly Jones, Tera Killip, Jenny Moussa Spring, and Maddy Wong for the expertise and guidance that make these books as wonderful as they are. We owe many thanks to our dynamic Feature Relations team, Stephanie Martinez-Arndt and Maura Turner, and to our legal eagles Serena Dettman, Laura Finell, and John Lomazzi, who stayed calm during the chaos while keeping track of all the details.

We are appreciative of Pixar's executives, Reema Batnagar, Lindsey Collins, Jonathan Garson, Chris Kaiser, Jim Kennedy, Steve May, Jim Morris, Tom Porter, Jonas Rivera, Katherine Sarafian, and Britta Wilson for supporting a story with such technical and artistic challenges. Thank

Maria Yi, *digital*

you for going to bat for us to get the resources we needed to complete the movie.

We owe a special thank-you to Alan Bergman, who advocated for the film from day one.

To Executive Producer Pete Docter, who is amazingly deft at imparting wisdom and guidance while simultaneously giving space for creative freedom and discovery; to Associate Executive Producers Mary Coleman, our champion from the very start, and McKenna Harris, who helped us to the finish line—we say thank you so very much.

To a truly phenomenal production team, Sanjay Bakshi, Krissy Cababa, Jesús Martínez, Becky Neiman-Cobb, and Danielle O'Farrell: You have been cherished partners from the beginning and contributed to the innovation and creativity required for every aspect of this mind-boggling film. You all made the journey jubilant and inspiring every single day. I am indebted to you for your partnership and friendship.

To the *Elemental* crew: This film has been a long journey, during which the world

dramatically changed. What both sustained us through the most challenging times and brought us joy was collaborating with such supremely talented people. Your spectacular artistry, the care you poured into every frame, and your unflagging commitment to making a great film are a wonder. You are the very best and brightest at Pixar, and we are profoundly grateful to you.

Denise Ream, Producer

Peter Sohn,
digital